HAPPY JESUS NURSE

Happy Jesus Nurse is about Redemption. It will take care of and help heal your heart.

—Jennifer Osteen, RN, Pastor's Wife, Lakewood Church

Baring her soul in this book, Anne Helton has given us a road map to use our own life lessons for spiritual and emotional healing.

—Dr. Susan Cooley, Nurse Practitioner

Overall, Happy Jesus Nurse *is a Love Story: Love of God, Family, and Marriage, and especially a story of God's love for us. This book is for all faiths and religions. Anne Helton finds a real relationship with Jesus without disparaging her Catholic roots or other people's faiths.*

—Monica Jones, M.Ed., School Teacher

Anne Helton offers a loving hand in a necessary walk inside your heart. Who are you as a spouse? Her pauses are real life; the lessons are critical: God, her coauthor, provides a beautiful spiritual dimension. Happy Jesus Nurse is *a most rewarding journey that you will want to revisit frequently.*

—U.S. Navy Captain (Retired), Joe Sullivan

Encouragement from Anne Stewart Helton

Genesis 50:20 tells us that anyone or anything meant to hurt us will be used for good but, my oh my, sometimes it seems to or does take a long time.

So, whatever you may be going through, don't give up!

HAPPY JESUS NURSE:
Heart Lessons

*Inspirational Stories and Lessons on Love,
Family, Marriage, Struggles and Recovery
from My Life Lived Backwards*

By Anne Stewart Helton, RN, BSN, MS

With "So, What Happened...? By John R. Helton, Sr.

ISBN 978-0-692-34564-1

Lace image on cover: www.dreamstime.com

Are you searching for meaning and purpose
from your own Life events? Do you ever feel mixed up
because you don't understand your circumstances?

✤

Do you need healing from a crisis, loss, betrayal,
estrangement, shame? Do you ever feel alone
or stuck in your healing?

✤

Is your Marriage struggling? Are you dealing
with pride, forgiveness, strongholds, or shame?
Is that holding you back?

✤

Is Recovery difficult? Do you find yourself
slipping back into negative behaviors
that hurt yourself or others?

✤

Do you want deeper spiritual relevance
in your life, regardless of your religion or background??

YOU ARE NOT ALONE AND YOU MATTER TO GOD!

DEDICATION

I dedicate this book to my soul mate, John-Bob Helton, who for over 50 years has walked with me through the natural and supernatural. You are a worthy man of God and you never gave up! Thank you. And much gratitude to my daughter Missy and friends Raquel and Martha, for their invitation to a Beth Moore home study Bible class and a referral to Lakewood Church, which eventually healed my heart.

ACKNOWLEDGMENTS

Special thanks to my smart, pretty, and wise daughter, Melissa Martin, "Missy", her fun and loyal husband, Larry, and my perfect grandchildren-Casey, Molly, Jack, and Matt-for their love, support, and excellent "heart lessons."

Thanks and hugs to the other Larry in my life, Larry Elliott, for forever friendship.

And also sending love and peace to my handsome, and very talented teacher, writer, artist son, John, Jr., "little Bobby," who will be in a treasured part of my heart forever, and also sending joy to his wife, Carisa.

Thanks to Dr. Susan Cooley, my nurse and photographer friend who was brave enough to read my first draft of *Happy Jesus Nurse* and tell me the truth. Susan lives life with joy and courage and is covered by GRACE.

Also thanks to *Happy Jesus Teacher*, Monica Jones, M.Ed., a spiritual woman with the gift of prophecy, and to *Happy Jesus Nurse*, Mother, Writer, and Spiritual Role Model for many people, Jennifer Osteen, for reading my stories and taking care of my heart. Special kudos to U. S. Navy Pilot (Ret.) Joe Sullivan and wife Sandy, for providing words of wisdom and support for this book and for getting us out of the "ditch."

Much gratitude to my daughter Missy and friends Raquel and Martha, for their invitation to a Beth Moore home study Bible class and a referral to Lakewood Church-Houston.

Heartfelt gratitude to Lakewood Church Pastors Joel and Victoria Osteen who helped heal our hearts and connected us to a living relationship with Jesus. Also to Ministers Clayton and Ashlee Hurst, Associate Pastor Paul Osteen, M.D. and wife Jennifer Osteen, Jon Swearingen and all the kind Lakewood Church staff, singers and volunteers who gave us hope and held our hands on our journey. And special smiles for Marriage Ministers Richard and Sheri Bright for providing laughter through any tears! Love and prayers to all of my Church family, who are walking the walk with Jesus, especially: Prayer Partner, Lynn Parks and husband Steve, sweet Odele Taylor and wise Barbara Bissett and her strong husband Baron, and prayer warrior Tammy Cascio and her supportive husband Pat. And to Mr. Anthony Perez who keeps us all safe and really dances well.

Love, honor and gratitude to my mother, Gerrie Stewart, who still encourages me, and my father, Emmett Stewart, and all my other ancestors who are in heaven watching over me.

Thanks to brother in-law, Dr. Mark Jacobs, for support and wisdom, my amazing nine siblings: Karen, Richard, Walter, Steve (in heaven), Cathy, Julie, Mary, Jimmy, and Billy; all of my in-laws and outlaws, as well as my brother-in-law, Dr. Bill Helton and his wife Lucille and sister in law Helen and her husband Joe Rhodes, for being supportive for many years. Blessings to my many friends who let me talk and listened with love, especially to my friend of 40 years, Sandy VandeGraaff and my Irish friend Kat.

Muchas Gracias for the heart lessons from my "California golden girl," cousin Kathy Clark Maxey, and my Super Happy Jesus Nurse friend: Melissa Smith Dover. You both helped me more than you'll ever know.

Feelings of thanks for Sheryl Burge at "Beautique Salon" in Houston

who listened to me for hours without judgment and kept me blonde when I wanted to dye my hair purple and to Marilyn O'Brien,RDH and Deborah Haase, DDS for keeping me relaxed and not grinding up all my teeth!!

Special Thanks to Michelle Prince and Prince Performance Group and for the design talents of Janet Long… you gave me courage!

You are all Blessed! ⚹

TABLE OF CONTENTS

INTRODUCTION
What Is a *Happy Jesus Nurse*?

By Anne Stewart Helton

Keep thy heart with all diligence; for out of it are the issues of life.
—Proverbs 4:23 (KJV)

W e all have life-healing moments and stories. My lessons have made me stronger and helped me fight through the storms of my life.

Some of my lessons have been wonderful, some glorious, some very painful, and some even tragic. Some moments in my life were seemingly meaningless at the time. So often we don't realize the importance of simple events until later in life or even until we feel it's too late—which is never. I have learned that being happy with Jesus is the key that unlocks the heart, no matter what your religion may be.

A Happy Jesus *Anyone* is someone who has the love of Jesus in their heart, someone who knows that HE is real and who then looks at people and life through the eyes of Jesus Christ. It sounds so simple and peaceful, but you know what? It's really hard!

I wasn't always a *Happy Jesus Nurse* or, in fact, a *Happy Jesus* anything! In years past, I was skeptical of people who said they were connected to Jesus. I did not understand or believe them. Being a *Happy Jesus Nurse*, for me, means that I look for healing on a variety of levels with myself and with others—physically, emotionally, and spiritually. Plus, I have the knowledge that Jesus is always available and that He is the source of comfort—He gives me strength when times are tough. He is my friend; He has my back; and He will keep me on track or get me back on track, whenever needed.

Keeping Jesus in one's heart makes it possible for one to be a *Happy Jesus Nurse,* or a *Happy Jesus* Photographer, Mother, Father, Friend, Salesperson, Landscaper, Actress, Barista, Engineer, Teacher, Lawyer, Physician, Writer, etc. It means you can live in PEACE by being prepared with God's Word to please God first and have healthy viewpoints and priorities, to remain loyal to those in your community, and thus give out encouragement and blessings to others who may be going through life's storms and experiencing grief, and to freely release all judgment, vengeance, pride, and hurt through forgiveness—thus receiving God's mercy and GRACE. The stories in this book represent this hypothesis.

The stories that follow describe some of my life moments, my Heart Lessons. They are meant to inspire you, encourage you, tweak you, and lead you to God, who will always give you health and healing.

As you read these *Heart Lesson* stories and consider the tips in this book, think about taking the challenge to examine your own life vignettes. If you are searching for deeper meanings of your life moments and ways to forgive yourself and others, review the situations that come to your own mind. Write a list of what surfaces in your thoughts—the good, bad and ugly. (You can always shred the list if you feel you need to!)

Write your own stories, knowing that it is often in the simplest of things or people in our events where you will gain insight, spiritual growth, and peace. Try to look for deeper meanings in everyday situations. Then, better still, create meaningful events every day. Think about instances that seem like "coincidences" in your daily life and find the links to what God may have laid out just for you.

Also, reading the Book of Proverbs helped me to bring my life together and change my heart. It may help you find Wisdom too.

As I sit today in a cardiac care waiting room, while my eighty-eight-year-old mom has a heart catheterization, I can't help but feel every prick she must be experiencing. I am just wired that way.

This is just another day of *Heart Lessons* for her, for me, and for our family; and I am confident that we will find great meaning. ⚜

The Happy Jesus Nurse
ENCOURAGEMENT

✦

That their hearts might be comforted, being knit together in love, and unto all riches of the full assurance of understanding, to the acknowledgment of the mystery of God, and of the Father, and of Christ.

—Colossians 2:2 (KJV)

"Where is the heart catheterization waiting room?" I asked the smiling lady in the gift shop. I should know this, having worked in the famous Texas Medical Center too many years ago, but my brain was fuzzy with stress today, and I craved coffee. I prided myself on being a *Happy Jesus Nurse*, but today I was more the *grumpy lost-child nurse*.

My almost-ninety momma had suffered a heart attack, and it needed mending. It started with a bump from her walker in her bathroom, a slight fall, complaints of minor hip pain, then a transport via ambulance to the emergency room (just in case). Then, as I and my sister Mary watched her being taken to x-ray on a gurney, she cried out in extreme pain, and we saw her clutch her head with her large veined hand. (Uh-oh, nurse, order a CAT scan too!) Sadly, right on cue, she grabbed her chest, which housed the biggest heart ever.

Wait! What? Thanks a lot, God. I get to watch my own mother have a heart attack!

Houston Fire Dept. Ambulances

I'm a registered nurse who trusts in Jesus, and I used to work in cardiac nursing. But it's not very often you watch a family member begin with one problem and then have a myocardial infarction (heart attack) right in front of your eyes. And, glory of glory, here we were in the hospital where presidents and kings go for health care. And here was my sweet momma trying not to bother anyone with her heart pain. In a soft voice, she said, "Yes, it hurts a little; maybe you could just give me something to help me breathe better, please?"

Oh, Lord, please help my momma.

※

My mother was born in the golden days, in 1926. She was a Los Angeles girl who relished life. I mean really! She was a classic good girl dressed in a uniform. She played sports and volunteered in the rectory at the Catholic girls' high school. Also, she was known to be seen sneaking out at night

Anne and Mother Gerrie

with her sisters to hear the real big band musicians. She was recruited by her Hollywood aunt to be in the movies. She spent time making bandages for the Red Cross during World War II. And she met the love of her life, my dad, Emmett Stewart, at a Loyola dance.

Hit by the thunderbolt, she married him at nineteen and proceeded to obey the Pope and have ten children. I was number one. Number two was ad-

Stewart Family (10 children)

venturous Karen. We were California born, and then eight more followed, in St. Louis and Houston—far away from Mom's home roots.

So, when I say she had a big heart, you can only imagine how big it had
to be for ten children. Her favorite saying was a joyful one: "What a Life!"

On this day of her heart catheterization, I thought about all the
times we had spent together, helping each other, mostly laughing,
sometimes crying, and rarely arguing. I thought about how unselfish
her life had been. She was and is really smart. She easily could have
gone to college and had a career. In fact, she went to nursing school
for a while. My sweet hubby helped her get in, encouraged her, and
drove her to classes at the old Hermann Hospital in the Texas Medical Center of Houston. She loved school. But that only lasted until my
dad needed knee surgery and wanted her home. Wives and mothers
did things like that then. To this day though she still uses her nursing
school knowledge!

During the '60s, it was my mother who took in stray friends of
ours, letting them live in our tree house for a night to cool down from
a family issue or feed them dinner before they went home to apologize to their parents. It was Mom who would drive the streets of our
neighborhood in her red station wagon, yelling out the window at the
early drug dealers who were invading our peaceful suburban struc-
ture. She watched in horror as drugs captured some of her loved ones,
and she fought like a warrior to stave it off.

It was Mom who went to choir practice late at night after all of
us were asleep so she could sing for the monsignor at High Mass on
Sundays. She had an angel's voice and could belt out a tune in church
for the Hallelujah, or with my dad on Saturday nights when they
danced a jitterbug to our giggles and screams for more.

It was Mom who would let us make burned popcorn—because we
looooved it!—even though it would smoke up our kitchen and make
my father groan. She let us put raw tortillas directly on a gas burner
to burn them too and splatter them with butter and salt. At Thanksgiving she would put a giant still half-feathered turkey in the kitchen

sink (they were cheaper) and let us spend hours pulling out the feathers! In the summer, she would wash freshly caught crabs from the bay and then cry with us as we dropped them in boiling water for dinner.

It was my mother who held my hand when I got pregnant at sixteen and didn't know what was wrong with me. And it was my mother who welcomed my teen husband to my life with open arms and support. I look back now at how hard that must have been—but Mom DID NOT JUDGE ME!

It was my mother who shared her hopes, dreams, disappointments, and pain with frankness, gentle truth, teaching, and lessons. She even managed joyful times as she walked beside my father when he was diagnosed with the long painful journey of Alzheimers. It was Mom who helped me get through painful times in my life by listening, loving, and encouraging.

OH, WHAT A GIFT!

⁂

So, as I watched the nurses take her into the cath lab, I knew the great physicians could not give her a completely fixed or even repaired heart, but I prayed for a mended heart. Mending is really stronger; it's different. It's like the mended socks my grandmother worked on long ago, or like the mended stitches on an old bed quilt. You can see them, they take up space; you can feel them, but they buy

Knarled "mended" tree

you time and are stronger sometimes than the sewing-machine seams. Sometimes mended socks will even have knobs on them and actually hold up better in the washing machine. A mended heart is like an old tree that can make it through another storm. It may be covered with bumps and knobs, but it is still standing, still strong for another storm.

Just before the nurses wheeled Mom into the pre-op room, she smiled at her all-grown children gathered around her bed like perched chicks and laughed a little with us, especially when Jim (#9) and Billy (#10) walked in and joked, telling her to get out of bed.

She told us her usual line: "It's okay. I'm ready to go—if it's my time." And she also said, "I'm going to kill your father when I see him for leaving first." That was always her favorite. After all, they had an incredible sixty-three-year marriage.

We kissed her and told her she would be fine and Julie, her #7 child, grabbed her strong hand with the red painted nails, one more time.

Julie holds Mom's hand

Just a little more time, *please*, Jesus!

Jesus answered our prayers. The cardiologist said that her mitral heart valve was pretty bad and he couldn't do anything for her valve, but that he had given her more medicine. He was amazed that at her age her heart attack was so small and her heart's coronary arteries were so wide open.

But we weren't!

When she awakened from a hard sleep that evening, she brought back my own *Happy Jesus Nurse* heart as she opened her eyes widely and said so seriously, "I'm still here?"

Yes, Mom, you're still here. Dad and Jesus can wait a little longer; we need you here too.

She had to struggle a few days to keep her eighty-eight-and-a-half-year-old mended heart going—some nightmares and memory issues were difficult, but as always Mom was grateful.

A nurse's aide would bring her juice unannounced, a physical therapist would hold her gently to walk, a kind housekeeper would talk about the "old days" while cleaning her hospital room, and always Mom thanked them and encouraged them. She could make you feel like her best friend—and the thing was, she meant it!

Even in the middle of the night when she was scared or had trouble breathing, she would compliment the caretakers for their work.

Her love was turned on 24/7. Just like Jesus.

What a gift she was to everyone who knew her or had just met her. My father always said that "she never met a stranger."

So, we have more time, and my grandson, her great grandson, Jack, a Texas A&M student, wheeled her back to her sunny, assisted-living room yesterday. As she was rolled by the hard-working, tired nurses and worn out patients, she did her usual, "Thanks so much for taking care of me. I'm going to tell your supervisor to give you all a raise."

Grandson Jack wheels "GiGi" from hospital

My always social and thankful mom. She may not have finished nursing school but she is the healer and the encourager. She is the one with the softest, kindest, mended heart.

You, my dear little Momma, are the real *Happy Jesus Nurse!*

🙣

Thy father and thy mother shall be glad, and she that bore thee shall rejoice.

—Proverbs 23:25 (KJV)

ENCOURAGEMENT

Definition:

- The expression and acts of giving approval and support (Princeton WorldNet)

- Encouragers value human relations more than being right, and they value people more than things (Cameron Miredeth, PhD, and Timothy Evans, PhD, "Encouragement," *Family Journal of Individual Psychology.* http://www.carterandevans.com/portal/images/pdf/article20.pdf)

Who comforteth us in all our tribulation, that we may be able to comfort them which are in any trouble, by the comfort wherewith we ourselves are comforted of God.
—2 Corinthians 1:4 (KJV)

TIPS:

- REACH OUT to all people, especially the broken, whenever possible, in everyday situations.

- USE KINDNESS, respect, grace, and wisdom with your words and expressions.

- LISTEN to people before speaking—hear their thoughts, ideas, and dreams.

- BE CONSCIOUS of your body language—you might be giving mixed messages.

- IF CORRECTIVE encouragement is needed with someone, do it in private. Don't seek an audience. Don't seek credit.

- ELIMINATE CONTROL. Be sparse with giving advice. People can often figure out their own solutions.

- REFER people to professionals if more in-depth encouragement is needed or if the person asks for more help.

25

- PEOPLE will remember your honest approach and how it made them feel.
- FIND THE POSITIVES—but no false praise.
- KEEP CONFIDENCES.

Wherefore comfort yourselves together, and edify one another, even as also ye do.

—1 Thessalonians 5:11 (KJV)

The $200 Salad
PREPAREDNESS

❧

But that on the good ground are they, which in an honest and good heart, having heard the word, keep it, and bring forth fruit with patience.

—Luke 8:15 (KJV)

"The dirt is ready!" My sweet, sweaty husband said to me, as he necessarily rested his much appreciated muscles. He had created a garden area six feet by sixteen feet in an unused part of our backyard. He had shoveled, weeded, and bordered it with perfect wood, and created a masterpiece in the ground. He stirred up earthworms to give them space to roam and he brought in organic soil to enrich the Houston clay. He had trimmed overhanging branches to let in the sun and measured everything just right so I could walk down the deck walkway to get my hands in the rich dirt. I bragged to anyone who would listen that I was going to feed us from now on with healthy, home-grown, rain-watered Texas foods. The dirt was ready. He had done the heavy lifting—but it was still my garden.

John prepares garden

It was my turn now. Get out of my way!

Oh, the sweetness of the tomatoes, bell peppers, basil, lettuce, green beans, squash, and cucumbers could already be tasted. Those pioneer women had nothing on me. I even planted potatoes that could be stored for the winter! I also had peach, fig, pear, and lemon trees scattered in the yard to provide plenty of vitamin C and natural sugars for our bounty. We could survive on our own if needed. After all Annie was in control—hmmm!

And out of the ground made the LORD God to grow every tree that is pleasant to the sight, and good for food; the tree of life also in the midst of the garden, and the tree of knowledge of good and evil.

—Genesis 2:9 (KJV)

I watched for buds in the soil every day. I proudly waited for the fruits of my labor.

My first clue that this might be another life lesson for me should have been the demise one day of one whole perfect row in my garden.

Each day, I couldn't wait to admire the multiple hills of seeds growing, but one morning I saw that a creature had rummaged through a row, and the row now looked wiggly and lumpy with seeds moved everywhere.

HEY! This is MY garden. Who or what did this?

I did everything right. I prepared and studied about vegetables. I designed this garden. I worked the soil. I planted the seeds! I told everyone about my garden.

Then my husband appeared behind me and said, "Wow! Why did you make that row crooked and lumpy?"

Wrong Day for a *WHY* Question!

What's the big deal? It's only a silly garden, I thought, as I pounded the crooked row straight again and tried to figure out which seeds went where. As I watered the dirt and saw some seeds and little plants wash away I felt like taking all the rows and mixing them up like a salad just to see what would grow where and what wouldn't.

Why in the world was I so upset about a garden not being perfect?

Then I looked over at my pear tree and saw that all the fading white flowers had black spots on them where the little pears should grow, and they were dropping quickly with each breath of the wind. What was happening? I quickly grabbed my super-duper organic sprayer, and without checking the direction of the wind, I doused all the tree limbs as high as my five-foot frame could reach. The windy dousing thus included my hair, mouth, and eyes, which were too stubborn by now to mind.

I then glanced at *my* fig tree. Now what could possibly go wrong with an "oh, so biblical" fig tree?

It was covered with bird poop! The very nerve! I feed those birds every day.

As my husband wisely watched from the window, I grabbed my hose to wash the fig tree down good, and while spraying the clean water on it, I flashed back to my gardens of the past—the days of watching my California grandfather pick oranges, avocados, and grapefruit from his backyard trees, and of hearing my father tell me to "hit" the fruit tree trunks to stress and trick them into blooming and then later seeing it actually come true!

I remembered my long-ago backyard potato and carrot patch that I planted with my children. I pictured my sweet, curly-haired, feisty daughter Melissa's waiting blue eyes as she pulled up the skinny carrot tops every day "just to see if there were any carrots yet." And I remembered my parents' joy when looking at my garden that was planted in Wimberley long before my dad began to forget. I remembered our son, little Bobby, digging and weeding just like his father had done to build me a garden in our first small shaky house, which looked like a castle to me! I remembered how proud Bobby was when the seeds grew real corn from his dirt.

I Never Thanked Him!

I thought about all the times I had perfectly planned and organized my own garden rows of life only to have the seeds scattered, be picked up by unexpected and angry birds, or just disappear with no explanation attached.

I felt shame—but relief!—as I realized once again that none of life is mine to control; not the dirt, not the rows, no matter how perfectly I plan, and certainly not the seeds or fruits of my labor. All are fleeting gifts from God as He allows us to work His soil in His garden. And Jesus stays by our side to walk with us as we learn the lessons we need to learn during our planted time here on earth.

I sat on the ground and let the water spray up on the fig tree and fall from my eyes, and I prayed:

Oh, God, it's Annie again. Thank you for letting me see and feel the seeds of my life, no matter how fleeting, and thank you for scattering and growing them as you see fit. Help me to keep my life in a row when I can, but mostly help me to appreciate the crooked lumps too, and help me to appreciate those who toil around me and help me.

This isn't MY Garden, it is yours; and if you scatter the seeds, I know you will plant them just where they need to grow and that they won't need my watchful eyes, "perfect" plans, or ever-working, controlling hands. They will always have yours.

In Jesus' name I pray. Oh, how I pray!

✲

And he said unto me, My grace is sufficient for thee: for my strength is made perfect in weakness. Most gladly therefore will I rather glory in my infirmities, that the power of Christ may rest upon me.
—2 Corinthians 12:9 (KJV)

Yes, perfect in our weakness.

Handful of tomatoes

Well, the garden looks to be flourishing now. Mostly just greens, radishes, and maybe a few tomatoes and cucumbers—actually, in truth, it is just a $200 salad.

But... If you look closely at the rows, you can see the scattered lettuce growing outside of them. It's growing better than the others because, finally, the dirt was ready! ❦

Scattered, growing lettuce

PREPAREDNESS

Definition:

- To make ready beforehand for a specific purpose, as for an event or occasion (Dictionary Search. Yahoo.com)
- To fit, adapt, or qualify for a particular purpose or condition; to make ready; to put into a state for use or application as to prepare ground for seed; to prepare a lesson—(Webster's Dictionary)

> *But sanctify the Lord God in your hearts: and be ready always to give an answer to every man that asketh you a reason of the hope that is in you with meekness and fear:*
>
> —1 Peter 3:15 (KJV)

TIPS (to prepare your "soil" for your SOUL):

- TO PRAY IS TO PREPARE. It may not seem like it, but it's a purposeful act of self-discipline to connect directly to God on a regular basis, instead of worrying like Martha and calling upon Him in crisis, with worry-like behavior; be more like Mary and use prayer. It will decrease your anxiety and your need to be in control.

> *And Jesus answered and said unto her, Martha, Martha, thou art careful and troubled about many things:*[42]
> *But one thing is needful: and Mary hath chosen that good part, which shall not be taken away from her.*
>
> —Luke 10:41–42 (KJV)

- REVIEW YOUR CORE VALUES AND BELIEFS. In any crisis they will be critical to sustain you and keep you connected to God. If you keep the Word of God inside you, then you will have it when needed!

• PRACTICE SCENARIOS IN YOUR MIND. Picture yourself in difficult situations or around difficult persons and realize that you cannot control that person or situation but you can control yourself. Prepare prayerful responses ahead of time.

• PEOPLE WITH A HIGHER SENSE OF PERCEIVED CONTROL OVER LIFE'S STRESSORS (PREPARED PEOPLE) show better health and less stress hormones (cortisol). You can't control other people and all situations but you can have more perceived control by being prepared. Let prayer be your preparation. Reduce your stress with prayer! (Chronic high stress levels effect memory and over time, your health. *Social and Health Factors That Impact Aging*, based on Lachman, 2006 and Miller & Lachman, 1999.)

• IT'S A PARADOX OF LIFE, BUT TO GAIN ALL WE MUST GIVE IT UP. Gain peace…Release your thoughts of control to Almighty God, and pray!

• YOUR MIND CONTROLS YOUR BRAIN, NOT THE OTHER WAY AROUND (Dr. Caroline Leaf, "Switch on Your Brain," © 2013, used by permission of the author) What you allow in your mind and soul will take root in your brain. Prepare your life for goodness and health, speak positive thoughts, read God's Word, and make wise choices. Don't be afraid to tell others the good news!

Preach the word; be instant in season, out of season;
reprove, rebuke, exhort with all long suffering and doctrine
—2 Timothy 4:2 (KJV)

Practice These Three Happy Jesus Nurse Tips Daily:

• SAY THIS DAILY PRAYER OF COMPLETE TRUST IN GOD EVERY MORNING:

O Lord, please help me to realize that nothing will happen to me today that You and I cannot work out together.

(*Catholic Book of Prayers,*
edited by Rev. Maurus
Fitzgerald, O.F.M., 2001)

- BE HONEST WITH YOURSELF, AS MUCH AS POSSIBLE, EVEN IF IT HURTS...OUCH!
- WHEN THINGS GET TOUGH DURING THE DAY—AND THEY WILL!—PUNT IT ALL BACK TO GOD!

For we are his workmanship, created in Christ Jesus unto good works, which God hath before ordained that we should walk in them.

—Ephesians 2:10 (KJV)

Just Like Lucy and Ethel
LOYALTY

A fool's mouth is his destruction, and his lips are the snare of his soul.

—Proverbs 18:7 (KJV)

"Friendship, Friendship…"

The song from Cole Porter and "I Love Lucy" was playing loudly over and over in my head when I hung up the phone. If we had been standing next to each other wearing the same dresses, we would have been ripping off each other's dress flowers just like the classic *Lucy and Ethel* skit on the *Ed Sullivan Show* long ago. My friend even had red hair!

We knew every button to push on each other's shoulder chips, and boy, were we pushing them—albeit through clenched teeth and high-pitched voices. We had been friends for more than thirty years, had gone to nursing school together, held the hands of sick and dying patients, loved talking about cardiac care, had been through child rearing, relationship issues, and all the roller-coaster ups and downs and curves that life could throw us. We could always be honest with each other. She could tell me my faults, and I would listen. I could listen and

"Friendship" dress and hat

advise her, and she would usually say, "Hmmm, that's a good point!" We could be that way with each other. But we had not talked much in several months. We each had busy lives and had only briefly checked in with each other for quick updates—always ending with, "We need to get together."

And then came the phone call: "Those people you work with always seem disorganized, you must have really changed to be able to stay there!" she said to me, knowing how proud I was to be working part-time again.

"Well, they are really supportive, so I am overlooking some issues," I responded defensively.

"It's a shame you can't just volunteer," she replied.

Okay, sister, I thought, and with barrels loaded I said, "Oh, how nice it is that you don't work in nursing anymore but what do you do all day? Your life must be so boring."

Her retort came before I was finished. "I don't HAVE to work. WE have plenty of money," she said, knowing my family had been through financial difficulties.

OUCH!

RIP OFF THOSE FLOWERS!

What were we doing? The verbal volley ended with "*FINE!*" and me hanging up. Sometimes I had trouble resolving confrontation. After the phone call I thought of all the words I could have said to my friend. None of them were kind. All of them were justification words for my feelings and to prove I was "right." All of my pretend words to her were from my own perspective, through my own filter. *What is wrong with her?*

This doesn't happen with my nurse friend Melissa and me!

A fool hath no delight in understanding, but that his heart may discover itself.

—Proverbs 18:2 (KJV)

But *she* was being the fool? Right? I should just stay away from people like her and forget her. But something inside me knew that I had taken her words personally and that we had hurt each other. This wasn't my first encounter with this issue, and deep down I knew I needed to work on it. Darn!

I needed to look in the mirror. I do get my feelings hurt, and I do "read" inferences into other people's words sometimes without clarifying. I do cover up my real feelings of fear, unworthiness, anger, and hurt, and then "hang up" on people verbally or physically. As I was talking to her, I was worried about starting a new job but didn't admit it. Her approach was tacky, but I was worried about money.

She called me back once, and I saw her number on my phone. I didn't answer it. Something must be going on inside her too. I prayed for peace about the issue and realized I had forgotten to seek God and stand in faith and love instead of acting on my own feelings about my friend.

Charity suffereth long, and is kind; charity envieth not;
charity vaunteth not itself, is not puffed up,
Doth not behave itself unseemly, seeketh not her own,
is not easily provoked, thinketh no evil,
Rejoiceth not in iniquity, but rejoiceth in the truth;
Beareth all things, believeth all things,
hopeth all things, endureth all things.

—1 Corinthians 13:4–7 (KJV)

It was months later and St. Patrick's Day. My friend, who was always the one I could count on to appreciate the old country, would ask about my grandmother, Mary Catherine O'Gallagher, from County Mayo, Ireland. She knew I was a Shenachie, an Irish and Scottish storyteller, but my friend actually used that word in her e-mails! My friend still believed in Fey—fate and whimsy. She had traveled back to Ireland, and she was adventurous, going once on a dog sled ride through Alaska. I was more cautious, I loved her stories, I was more fearful of travel. We both used old words of Gaelic origin sometimes in our discussions, like the hubbub of politics and having lived in shanties when we were first married. She taught me Irish sayings such as "Many a time a man's mouth broke his nose!" Her children even had Irish names!

Country hills

I remembered another old Irish saying: "If you're looking for a friend without fault, you will be without a friend forever." It was St. Patrick's Day. I picked up the phone.

"Oh, Hi," she said softly.

"Happy St. Patrick's Day," I said.

She answered, "I knew you would call me; I'm so glad. I just got home from the last cancer treatment." Her teenage daughter...I didn't know... And then we both cried.

After the call, I got out my old Rosary from my Irish grandmother and I got down on my knees and thanked God for always leading our hearts in the right direction, toward real friendship.

We were different, thankfully, but we still had "Friendship, Friendship." ✿

LOYALTY

Definition:

• The state or quality of being loyal; unswerving in allegiance; faithful to a private person to whom fidelity is due. (Webster's Dictionary)

• Not a "blind" following; i.e., not loyal to a fault, but a trusted loyalty.

He that is faithful in that which is least, is faithful also in much: and he that is unjust in the least is unjust also in much.

—Luke 16:10 (KJV)

A friend is someone who walks into a room when everyone else is walking out.

—Gary Moore

TIPS:

• BE SUPPORTIVE OF FRIENDS (OR FAMILY MEMBERS) not for any quid-pro-quo but just because. You might learn something about yourself. Try to identify your friend's needs, not what you may gain in the relationship.

• USE THE *Happy Jesus Nurse* **L.I.K.E.** PRINCIPLE:
   ○ LISTEN FIRST.
   ○ INTUIT: Try to hear deeper meanings.
   ○ KINDNESS RULES (even in a disagreement).
   ○ EMPATHIZE: Feel what your friend is feeling.

• THE NO GOSSIP RULE MUST APPLY—ALWAYS! Don't repeat information! Other people will tempt you, even bait you, like sharing some juicy gossip with you first just to get you going—don't bite!

• RESPECT YOUR FRIENDS' PRIVACY AND DECISIONS. You never know exactly what someone is going through.

- SOMETIMES YOU JUST NEED TO "BE THERE" quietly, and not even talk!
- SOMETIMES YOU NEED TO CLEAR THE AIR with a confrontation, apology, or an honest confession—Honesty builds trust, which is critical for loyalty.
- ONCE YOU'RE IN A TRUSTED FRIENDSHIP, share honestly with each other—This will build bonds!
- REMEMBER: DISLOYALTY and delighting in a person's misfortune or mistake IS DIFFICULT TO UNDO. Once trust is violated, it can take a long time—if ever—to regain.
- DISLOYALTY CAN EVEN BE AS HORRIBLE AS THE "CURSE OF HAM"!

And the sons of Noah, that went forth of the ark, were Shem, and Ham, and Japheth: and Ham is the father of Canaan.[19]
These are the three sons of Noah: and of them was the whole earth overspread.[20]
And Noah began to be an husbandman, and he planted a vineyard:[21]
And he drank of the wine, and was drunken; and he was uncovered within his tent.[22]
And Ham, the father of Canaan, saw the nakedness of his father, and told his two brethren without.[23]
And Shem and Japheth took a garment, and laid it upon both their shoulders, and went backward, and covered the nakedness of their father; and their faces were backward, and they saw not their father's nakedness.[24]
And Noah awoke from his wine, and knew what his younger son had done unto him.[25]
And he said, Cursed be Canaan; a servant of servants shall he be unto his brethren.

—Genesis 9:18–25 (KJV)

Washateria Wisdom
COMMUNITY

⁕

And the LORD said unto Moses, Go unto the people, and sanctify them today and tomorrow, and let them wash their clothes.

—Exodus 19:10 (KJV)

⁕

"I'm going to the Washateria," I said, while grabbing the two baskets of dirty clothes to put in my car. The washing machine had crashed and would need to be replaced. My helpful husband wanted to go with me but I wanted to experience this event in 2014 style. I had not been to a Washateria in many, many years, and I wanted to go all a-l-o-n-e.

So, I whisked up the basket, the soap, a bag of quarters, and a book to read, and I flew out the door. It seems silly but I…well, I was excited!

⁕

The Washateria on Eleventh Street was the place to go when I first married a million years ago. It was the Houston Heights in the early sixties, and it was rare to have a washer and dryer in my circle. In fact, having enough dimes and nickels to wash clothes was sometimes rarer. Often I could only wash the clothes—fifteen cents—and then would take the load home to dry them on a clothesline. It worked. It was a real luxury to have a quarter to dry the clothes too. If I had an extra dime I could get a coke; that was a treat. The center was noisy and crowded with big old humming ceiling fans. It had wrinkled newspapers to read, jobs posted on cork bulletin boards, and children running around everywhere. I could learn a lot about parenting by just watching the families around me. It was alive!

"Little Bobby", 1963

I was sixteen years old. I would bundle up my chunky baby boy in his stroller and put the laundry basket of diapers and towels on top of the stroller. It had a fancy little canopy above the seat which made me feel proud to push it. Being just five feet tall myself, it was a cumbersome push. In the stroller I had my bouncing baby Bobby and an unbalanced laundry basket on top as I toddled down broken sidewalks toward the welcoming sign of the Washateria. I did this several times a week. I even dressed up to go!

Sometimes I washed his diapers and little shirts in the bathtub, if needed. A family member gave us a washing machine once and we hooked it up in the kitchen. It never really worked, but it was fun because I had to sit on top of it to keep it from walking across the kitchen floor.

When I would arrive at the Washateria back then, I met mostly older mothers washing baskets of clothes. Every now and then, a teenage mom like me would be there; we would see each other, stare, and try to talk. I guess I was lonely, but I didn't know it at the time. I covered up that feeling well.

So did my teen hubby as he took his eighteen-year-old self to the grown-up world of men working at steel companies, oil fields, and street deliveries, pretending to be older than his years, wherever work could be found. It was the way to survive. He did that well.

And whatsoever ye do, do it heartily, as to the Lord, and not unto men.

—Colossians 3:23 (KJV)

⁂

The first thing I noticed when I arrived at the new Century Washateria this day was the number of men who were washing clothes. Hmmm?! Maybe I should have had my guy go with me! The machines were all different sizes—huge, shiny, and quiet. Everything was so very clean too.

The machines were so different that I had no idea how to operate them or how much a wash load cost. So, I watched the people around me. Most of them spoke Spanish, and the men were watching soccer on flat-screen TVs mounted on the wall. Little children ran around their parents' legs back and forth to the game machines. Some folks had iPads and some were texting on their phones. EVERYONE had a soft drink or coffee.

Boy, this would have really been fun those many years ago.

I put a load of clothes in the front-loading machine and had to stand on the step to see the top. The money slot was not clear and I must have looked pretty dumbfounded because a smiling lady came up to one side of me and a man to another and both asked if they could help.

To the lady I said *Yes*, and to the man I said *Si*.

I almost fell off the step when they told me that to wash one load of clothes was $4.50.

They laughed at my shocked face. Well, it just so happened I had brought a bag of coins.

I loaded up the machine with the soap and the money and sat down to wait.

The people around me were busy and happy. Their lack of expensive clothing was evident, and some dropped off their baskets of dirty clothes from banged up cars, but they were there cleaning and preparing their family garments for another day. We all were.

A young mother sat next to me with what seemed to be a four-year-old boy who was sweetly begging her for more money to buy some machine candy and a toy. She gave in and he was back in seconds for more. She said, "Last time," and handed him a few more coins; he took off only to return quickly again. I watched closely to see how she would handle him.

He was a master. He told her how good he had been at home, how he had picked up his toys and eaten all his lunch. She smiled and nodded, telling him she was proud of him for doing all of that. Then he thought a bit and came in from a different angle. "I'm your best little boy," he said. And she agreed. Then he said, "And you should give me more money."

She said NO—just that one word—"*NO*." Not with an explanation of not having any more money, not with shame or a promise of "another time," not with an explanation of dinner time coming, or a bribe of something else at home. Not even with a scowl or raised voice. JUST A NO!

> *But let your communication be, Yea, yea; Nay, nay: for whatsoever is more than these, cometh of evil.*
>
> —Matthew 5:37 (KJV)

Now, how in the world did that young mother know how to do that? I never got that right. In fact, my super nurse friend, Susan, recently reintroduced that concept to me with a clear directive, "Anne, you need to mean what you say and say what you mean. If you mean yes, say it; and no, say that. Everything else is confusion!"

Oh my! The Washateria momma's little one screamed and held his breath when he realized his tears and manipulative words wouldn't work. His momma just patted him on the head and started folding her clothes fresh out of the dryer. The little guy fell to the floor and stomped his feet, but I noticed he would glance his eyes her way, checking her response every now and then.

I watched in amazement at her resolve.

I still have trouble saying NO as an adult. In fact, I find myself sometimes offering excuses or rationalizing points with my answers to family or friends thinking I might hurt someone's feelings if I said NO to something. But really, I just want everyone to like me. It took me a long time to figure out that it was important to like myself too!

I thought about the scripture from Matthew and about how important it was to have boundaries in life. I remembered other strong, good women in my life, my mother-in-law, Maxine, in particular. She could be assertive and sometimes curt, but she was honestly always clear. People knew where they stood with her because she knew where she stood.

Maxine Helton,
mother in law

I could tell that this Washateria mom was at peace with her parenting boundaries, and I thought how blessed she was.

I wanted to bottle up her resolve and sell it!

Can you imagine a world where we all are honest about saying *Yes* when we mean yes and *No* when we mean no? Especially if it's said with kindness, and especially if it's filtered through good choices of God's plans for us and not our own.

It was time to put my clothes in the dryer, and I hadn't read one page of my book. I pulled the wrung-out wet clothes from the fancy washing machine and found the closest dryer, which happened to be right next to the young mother. She was still folding her clothes on the tall wooden table. I felt compelled to talk to her, just like moms talked to me so many years ago.

"You are a great mother," I said.

She seemed surprised, and I wasn't sure if I had stepped over a boundary of hers. Then her eyes relaxed but were teary.

"It's hard sometimes," she said. "His daddy left us, but I'm trying to do what's right."

I took a deep breath and was going to offer lots of "older woman" words of comfort with unasked for advice, but—Thank you, Jesus for holding my often-too-quick tongue— she continued:

"Yes, his daddy left us, but his spiritual Father in heaven is always with us , and I call on HIM and when I try to figure out what to do. I read this." She patted a well-worn Bible sitting by her purse. She smiled as she glanced over at her son who was talking to another little boy and had forgotten all about the candy. "He's a good boy, and we even pray for his daddy every night." A special *heart lesson* for sure.

I said nothing and just listened as she told me her only too familiar story of being a teen mom, working during the day, attending school at night, and trying to make a better life for her child. I listened to her describe her challenges with money and how she had taken a bus to the Washateria. None of it was complaining; it was just a young mom talking, until I heard my dryer bell *ding*.

"Your clothes are already dry," she said. She smiled and pointed.

I gathered my clothes into the basket.

As I was leaving the Washateria, I noticed I still had a couple of dollars of quarters in my plastic bag. I asked the mom if I could give the bag to her, for her son. She thought a minute and said, "Well, that's really nice, but you can give him the money, not me. I already told him no more!" We both smiled at each other.

I wondered just how great her son would turn out in life with a momma like her!

After a quick "Thank you" from the little boy, I noticed over my shoulder how fast he ran to the candy machines to spend the few quarters. I laughed and thought about how going to the Washateria should be a required field trip in schools and parenting classes.

As I glanced back at the young mother folding more clothes, I wondered what in the world God had planned for this wise young Washateria woman I had just met.

She will be in my prayers.

For I know the thoughts that I think toward you, saith the LORD, thoughts of peace, and not of evil, to give you an expected end.

—Jeremiah 29:11 (KJV)

Oh, also, I have a new washer now—darn! ⚜

Anne's new washer

COMMUNITY

Definition:

- Community can be geopolitical, like a specific neighborhood or city, or it can be phenomenological, that is a relational or interactive group. People who share an identity, culture, values, interests, and/or goals. (Mary Neis & Melanie McEwen, "Community Public Health Nursing, 2011).

> *And let us consider one another*
> *to provoke unto love and to good works:*[25]
> *Not forsaking the assembling of ourselves together,*
> *as the manner of some is; but exhorting one another:*
> *and so much the more, as ye see the day approaching.*
>
> —Hebrews 10:24–25 (KJV)

- YOU are part of your community. Whatever you do always makes a difference, in some way.

- It's actually mathematical and orderly. You are part of life's equations and with good choices and behaviors, you can influence a positive outcome. You are a variable in the equation toward a God-centered community.

TIPS:

The *Happy Jesus Nurse* Equation:

- $Y \times P = G2$

- Y (YOU) times P (ANOTHER PERSON) = G2 (GOD squared— A GOD CENTERED COMMUNITY)

> *Every action in our lives touches on some chord that will vibrate in eternity.*
>
> —Edwin Hubbel Chapin

- CREATE WAYS TO MAKE A DIFFERENCE. In community health we talk about "upstream thinking." Try to figure out "why" people are hurting and falling in a river of problems (yourself included); then go upstream and try to prevent them and yourself from falling into that river in the first place!

- FIND AND FOCUS ON THE CHOICES (Small and large) that you can make each day when you connect with others in your community—from a smile at the grocery store, a "wave in" for someone in traffic, meeting a newspaper man on the street. For years now, my husband has given several dollars to a newspaper man working extra for his family. He never takes a paper so the man can sell it to someone else. Now we know the man, ask about his children, and talk about the weather—we talk quickly though, at the traffic light! But it makes our community sweeter.

- USE THE GIFTS YOU HAVE. Everyone has some gift; volunteer in the community. You will gain more than you give. How about a monthly dinner where you invite people into your home for pot luck, people who have less than you? Or: Transport people receiving cancer treatments to church. Or: plan a Senior Sunday and volunteer in a senior center. (For ideas, AARP, 2014, CreateTheGood.org)

- JUST DO IT ALL WELL, and to God be the glory!

A new commandment I give unto you, That ye love one another; as I have loved you, that ye also love one another.[35]
By this shall all men know that ye are my disciples, if ye have love one to another.

—John 13:34–35 (KJV)

- AND REMEMBER: when dealing with people and groups in your community:

People don't care how much you know until they know how much you care.

—John Maxwell

"They're Not Happy"
BLESSINGS

❄

He that trusteth in his riches shall fall; but the righteous shall
flourish as a branch.

—Proverbs 11:28 (KJV)

"They're not happy," my dad said with a wink as he pointed to a block-long house in River Oaks, Houston's historically elite neighborhood. It was all meant to imply that we were happy, even with little money. Mom rolled her eyes, as she did every year when he said the same thing. It was the late 1950s, early '60s, and as usual Mom had little ones' feet jumping up and down on her lap. "Well, maybe they're just a *little* happy," she mumbled.

The first mansion in front of us was covered in blinking, colored lights and had wooden reindeers with a waving Santa perched on the chimney. This house also played blaring Christmas carols that entered our rolled-down car windows as we sang along with spirit. It was our yearly ritual during Houston's December season. Mom and Dad would gas up the red station wagon and all ten children would pile into the car, fighting over who got a window—which was numerically impossible.

My father adored this part of Christmas. He loved to entertain us while teaching us a lesson. It was a mixture of commercial fun and a "Las Posadas." Sometimes it was looking at the historic downtown

Foley's Department Store's Christmas window, and often it was spending three hours at
midnight Mass, but it was always special This
particular holiday was going to be different, but
we didn't know it yet.

Dad had asked us to go through our toys
and backyard corners and gather whatever we
didn't want or need. Now, this was actually
more difficult than one might imagine as we

Maxine's painted Santa

didn't really have "*toys*" like most of our friends, because there were
so many of us and we didn't have spare money. But we did have some
chipped, well-worn balsam-wood airplanes, paper dolls with homemade paper clothes, half-colored coloring books and broken crayons,
smudged cloth dolls, a variety of taped-together wooden guns, and
some half-aired-up balls. We also put together some old clothes, and
Mom made her famous sand tart cookies carefully wrapping them in
waxed paper. Somehow we had all of this packed in the station wagon
under a few jumping kids. This was before seat belts!

We must have looked funny hanging out of the car windows,
oooohing and ahhhing at the large homes, but we felt special. The
boys pointed to a HUGE black limo-type car parked in one driveway,
saying how much they wanted one just like it one day.

Like a tour guide on a bus, our Dad would describe to us the journey a very pregnant Mary and protective Joseph had taken through
Bethlehem and how they had looked everywhere for a place to stay.
We would laugh and say things like, "I wonder if these rich folks
would let them stay in their houses, if it were today?"

And Joseph also went up from Galilee, out of the city of Naza-
reth, into Judaea, unto the city of David, which is called Bethle-
hem; (because he was of the house and lineage of David:)[5]
To be taxed with Mary his espoused wife, being great with
child.[6] And so it was, that, while they were there, the days were

accomplished that she should be delivered.[7] And she brought forth her firstborn son, and wrapped him in swaddling clothes, and laid him in a manger; because there was no room for them in the inn.

—Luke 2:4–7 (KJV)

Just about when we had a definite divide in our thoughts about "rich versus poor," wisely my parents' lessons would shift. Dad would tell us his favorite saying about the importance of never judging anyone until you walked a mile in their shoes, new shoes or ones with holes in them and how it didn't matter whether you were rich or poor or in-between, it was always about the richness of your heart and how you treated people.

Maxine's painted Nativity

He would describe about how once his best friend was very wealthy and had helped many big families without food or clothing and also about how poor people he knew would share their lunch sandwiches with co-workers, if someone was hungry. He talked a lot about *"treasures of the heart,"* which none of us totally understood at the time.

> *But lay up for yourselves treasures in heaven,*
> *where neither moth nor rust doth corrupt,*
> *and where thieves do not break through nor steal:[21]*
> *For where your treasure is, there will your heart be also.*
>
> —Matthew 6:20–21 (KJV)

So, after the glitz and glitter of looking at Christmas lights for hours, we drove away from the fancy neighborhood that December night, thinking we were on our way home, forgetting we still had bags of goodies in the car. *But My Parents Remembered!*

Dad turned northwest and drove down a winding, dusty, bumpy road. He stopped the car in front of several barely-lit small houses. We could see shadows of men working on a pile of worn bricks off the road, even in the darkness. They stopped as we drove up. Brothers Richard (#3) and Walter (#4), called it "The Brickyard." They became more serious, their kind hearts had helped here before. When my dad got out of the car, the tall man waved. They exchanged greetings in Spanish. He knew Dad! It was a little scary, but somehow it felt safe. I can't explain it. Our eyes were large as we watched some older women, young mothers, and babies exit their homes. Then a group of children, one for each of our ages it seemed, came out of a house. As the door opened we could see a Christmas tree in the room with some worn decorations that I swear looked vaguely familiar. Even strings of popcorn were hanging on the tree, just like at our house.

Dad instructed us all to get out of the car and hand out the toys, clothes, and Mom's cookies. We went to work, eyeing up each child that came into our view. Little sister Mary (#8), smiled as she handed over a favorite doll. There were lots of *thank yous* and *gracias*, but mostly we were quiet with moist eyes. I could feel the tugs at my heart. My mother hugged the other mothers, and then we piled back into the station wagon. As the car started up we hung out of the windows, saying "Merry Christmas!" to all. And my Dad was bellowing out his car window, "Feliz Navidad!" He spoke great Spanish.

We drove down the worn brickyard road quietly thinking about the visions of the night, the beautiful lights of the River Oaks homes and the beautiful stars of the brickyard's night sky. My Dad pulled the station wagon over to the side of the road to let a car drive by us. Heading toward the worn houses was a long, beautiful black limo-type car, full of children and bags of toys, driving right by us. They were hanging out of the windows too, just like us. They waved and we waved back to them, we turned around and watched as they pulled up to the same houses.

We were all connected to each other, all connected in the treasures of our hearts.

It was Christmas. It was love. It was a forever lesson to never judge.

I used many of the same lessons with my own children—many times to their yawns and rolling eyes too. As parents, we would take little Bobby and Missy to donate toys and clothes, sometimes putting boxes of toys anonymously on porches on Christmas Eve so the parents of those children could be Santas too. We even put wrapping paper in the box for the parents to use. We passed on many of the same traditions we received from my parents. For example, every Thanksgiving our grandchildren help us make turkey dinners, and we hand out plates to groups of men waiting to find work on the holiday so they can feed their families.

And sometimes our treks turn out funny, like when we found a family reported to be in dire need; we went to their house to find out they had rooms and rooms of donated goods.

Oh well, they will give them to someone else, we decided.

Usually, if our children—and now grand-children—ever complained about someone, we would remember to say, "Until you've walked a mile in their shoes…." Or, if they didn't feel well and whined, my retort was often, "Do you know how many really sick and hungry children there are out there?"

Grandson Matthew and Anne prepare turkey dinners

Always ready to give a heart lesson, but often needing to learn my own.

Recently I was driving with my daughter Missy to a trendy eatery in one of Houston's "perfect" neighborhoods. She saw a friend's huge house and was commenting about the extraordinary exterior, large beautiful landscaping, and saying how nice it would be to have an extra bedroom and bath for her four children.

I couldn't help it, and I said with a wink, "But they're not happy."

She rolled her eyes at me and said, "Well, maybe they're just a *little* happy, Mom." And we laughed.

Then she looked at the large house and back at me and said, "Maybe they've read Matthew 6 too, Mom, and maybe they know, '*For where your treasure is, there your heart will be also.*' Maybe they share their **extra** blessings *all the time*, Mom! So, then yes, yes, they are happy!"

Ouch! Thank you, Jesus, for that lesson about not judging others—rich or poor!

My wise daughter is right again! And she and husband Larry continue to live Christianity by speaking truth, blessing others and passing on the best lessons to their children with great Catholic School education and love.

Dear Lord, it's me, Annie, again! Help me to see people through your eyes. Remind me frequently that what MY heart is focused on will become what I see and seek. Help me to seek YOU first in all things. Amen

Martin Family (Molly, Casey, Jack, Larry, Missy and Matthew)

BLESSINGS (Sharing)

Definition:

- A special favor, mercy or benefit
- Something promoting or contributing to happiness, well-being or prosperity
- SHARING. To participate in, use, enjoy or experience jointly or in turns. (Dictionary Search.yahoo.com)

> *But to do good and to communicate, forget not: for with such sacrifices God is well pleased.*
>
> —Hebrews 13:16 (KJV)

TIPS:

- SHARING BLESSINGS will double the joy of your own blessings! Research shows that "giving makes you happier." (Journal of Research in Personality...by Michael Steger, University of Louisville, in *Live Science*, 2007).

- WHENEVER POSSIBLE, SHARE WITHOUT AN AUDIENCE or seeking credit. Put yourself in the receiver's shoes; spread joy without creating feelings of embarrassment or any expectation of gratitude. You may never see the results of your kindness, but the recipient may call upon the memory of your acts over and over for hope.

- IF YOU FEEL JUDGMENTAL ABOUT SOMEONE IN NEED, JUST SAY TO YOURSELF OR SAY OUT LOUD: "There but for the grace of God go I." Often, wrong decisions have put someone in a negative situation, but we have all made bad decisions. Perhaps by sharing your blessings—your gifts of time, money, goods, skills, hugs and smiles, and prayers—it will turn a person's life around.

- KEEP DAILY NOTES OF YOUR OWN BLESSINGS. Think of at least one of your own blessings every day!

• THE ULTIMATE FORM OF GIVING THANKS TO GOD FOR YOUR OWN BLESSINGS IS IN GIVING SERVICE TO OTHERS.

Often, your blessings will come from trials, and you will thus be more empathetic to others who are hurting. You will then be able to share your thanks and blessings even more.

Give, and it shall be given unto you; good measure, pressed down, and shaken together, and running over, shall men give into your bosom.

For with the same measure that ye mete withal it shall be measured to you again.

—Luke 6:38 (KJV)

Rich in Relevance
PLEASERS

᪥

To every thing there is a season, and a time to every purpose under the heaven.

—Ecclesiastes (KJV)

I was at a restaurant recently, standing by a group of seniors leaning on their walkers and canes. I heard them ask the young waitress about parking areas by the eatery. The woman laughed at them and said, "Well, isn't that irrelevant to you now?" Well, by the time the group left, that worker heard an earful about their years of excellent driving records, abilities, and spending power!

But it really made me think. Have you ever felt irrelevant? Well, I have.

It has become increasingly apparent as I have crossed the "middle-age" years now how important relevance is. When someone is relevant, it means they matter—they are important to people, to an issue or a situation. And, sometimes without feeling relevant we fear becoming rejected or throwaways. Sadly, this can happen especially as we age. Relevance gives us connectedness to others.

Sunset on Galveston Island

To our families.

To our world.

Often, relevance is seen paired in quid-quo-pro relationships. I become relevant only if I can give you something, or vice versa. As I have become older, I have noticed it becoming more difficult to feel relevant in a variety of situations. In the past, my relevance was usually tied to my roles—being a perfect wife, a good mother, the oldest sibling, a registered nurse.

I even feel left out sometimes now as I read some of my favorite writers or bloggers; they describe their everyday lives and troubles as being filled with wonderful or willful small children, stretching or grumpy adolescents, or graduating young adults who bring tears to their eyes. I remember those days clearly, but I feel the shakiness, the shift, of being in another season now.

However, I still find that I crave meaning in my everyday life, meaning that helps me to feel relevant. But my children are grown, my siblings are on their own, my career is part-time—does that make sense?

Once, in a very dark time of my life, I felt disconnected to people I loved—people I had placed my trust in forever. I felt hurt and rejected. I felt so alone. And I remember planning and plotting ways to reconnect or to feel relevant to them again.

How could I get them to need or want me? But the real or imagined rejection was too strong. Mostly, I was in a different season, and my planning only made things worse. Looking down, down into that low spot was uncomfortable but necessary. My prayers finally helped me begin to look up. I saw the joy of Jesus, and I felt HIS love for me. I didn't have to prove anything to God. I didn't have to connect with favors, or advice, or a special role, or things. I didn't even have to put anyone else down to lift me up. The veil of human relevance disappeared. I just had to accept HIS unconditional love and realize it is about the relevance of God in my life, not me. And that's all I needed to be relevant.

I have listened in quiet stillness to this message of love and heard deep in my soul that the key to relevance in our natural life is humble SERVICE. The more I can serve others in my earthly stay, the more I feel relevant to God's will for me. I don't have to make a big splash or even be noticed doing a good deed. I just try every day to make someone else feel better and to be thankful for the opportunities that God puts in front of me.

I know that I am wired to be creative—to "do stuff"—and not just observe life. But I also realize that I must stop and pray first to hear in my spirit what God wants me to do. Thus, my reach for relevance will be linked to Him first and not to what is relevant to others or to my desire to please others. When I do that, I feel PEACE; and then I feel an amazing clarity and energy, and I can do even more!

It's like the movie, *It's a Wonderful Life*—really! It's a great thing that we were all born.

If you don't believe that, just observe your own life for a few days and note the small differences you make: as you let someone go in front of you in a traffic lane; as you smile at the bagger in the grocery store checkout line, as you give up the best parking space at the mall, as you play peek-a-boo with a baby in his mother's arms to calm him down, or as you hand the (probably pretending) homeless man on the street a dollar. Watch how you smooth out the lines on your spouse's tired forehead with a smile after he's had a difficult day or, better still, after an argument. See how your elderly parent or neighbor beams when you pop in for a visit, "just because."

Write a note to a friend.

Call a sick neighbor.

Write a journal or a blog.

This is your time—this is always your time!

And who knoweth whether thou art come to the kingdom for such a time as this.

—Esther 4:14 (KJV)

It's all relevant. You are relevant to all. Every day walk through that door. You are always rich in relevance to God. 🌿

Anne's front door

PLEASERS
(Pleasing people rather than pleasing God)

Definition:

- PEOPLE PLEASERS lack confidence and seek approval from others; they are always worrying about what others think of them in order to feel needed or relevant.

- WE WOULD GET NOWHERE WITHOUT SOME PEOPLE-PLEASING BEHAVIOR, but there is a balance to be found between "being liked" and healthy, honest behavior. People pleasers fail because you can never please all the people, all the time. If you try to people please all the time, that behavior can become a vicious cycle of false sacrifice of the self, then feelings of failure or martyrdom, and then more attempts to please others. Obsession can follow as the pleaser tries to find the "buttons" to press to please others. What follows is a loss of self, a failure to meet your own needs because you are no longer even aware of them (addictions.org).

- PEOPLE PLEASING is called "NEEDING AN APPROVAL FIX" by Joyce Meyer in her book *The Approval Fix* (http://www.joyce-meyer.org/, used by permission of the author).

- IT'S REALLY SIMPLE: If we put other people and things first, we will forget the first commandment every time:

> *I am the LORD thy God,*
> *which have brought thee out of the land of Egypt,*
> *out of the house of bondage.[3]*
> *Thou shalt have no other gods before me.*
>
> —Exodus 20:2–3 (KJV)

PERIOD! AMEN! It is very clear!

TIPS:

- The sooner you develop your direct connection to God through prayer, reading the Bible, and daily discipline, the sooner you will avoid the pitfalls of feeling at the mercy of other people's approval for relevance.

- In every season of your life you are already "qualified" by God.

- It's important and okay to identify and acknowledge your own gifts, talents, desires, and values. Then when you connect with the important skills inside of you and ask the Holy Spirit to guide you, your steps will always remain relevant.

When trying to discern whom you are trying to please, develop some quick answers to these *Happy Jesus Nurse* self-exam questions:

A. *Why* am I doing this behavior? (Whatever behavior is in question: at work, with family, for pleasure) Try to watch your own behavior (as carefully as you do others!)

B. *How* does what I am doing make me feel? (Fulfilled, peaceful, proud, competitive, tired, ashamed, secretive, lost, alone)

C. *Who* am I depending on to see me doing this? (Whatever this is.)

D. *How* will I feel and *what* will I do when this period/season of my life is over? *What* have I put off to do *this*? (When this season or project is over, children are grown, career is over, fame is gone, wrinkles develop, or money is less, will I have regrets?)

E. Try to examine your motivation....ask yourself when making behavioral choices, even small ones: *How can I put God first in this choice?*

REMEMBER: In life, people will let you down but God never changes and JESUS is available 24/7. Put God first; bring your tithes and offerings to God, not people.

For I am the LORD, I change not;
therefore ye sons of Jacob are not consumed.

—Malachi 3:6 (KJV)

Rose-Colored Eyes
VIEWPOINT

꙳

Thou hypocrite, first cast out the beam out of thine own eye; and then shalt thou see clearly to cast out the mote out of thy brother's eye.

—Matthew 7:5 (KJV)

"*imi, I think I was born with rose-colored eyes*," my blue-eyed, six-year-old granddaughter whispered to me.

My, oh my! What a profound statement—but mostly, what a profound concept!

She went on to explain, as best she could, "You know how some people have rose-colored glasses and are happy? I think I have rose-colored eyes."

Granddaughter Molly Martin

She had been struggling with a silly little-girl argument with her group of school friends and she was trying desperately to understand each of the girls' position on the issue. She kept explaining to all the girls everyone's feelings. She was becoming frustrated because she "got it," and they all seemed to want to keep arguing—thus her insight that *she* must be different.

She was different. She had the natural ability to

be positive and empathetic—both traits being a curse and a blessing in today's world.

She knew instinctively that God does not condemn us. Instead, he sends the Holy Spirit to convict us. It's confusing but real. When something goes wrong or we do something wrong, God's way is to teach us about the error and then give us the strength or "spirit" to change, to apologize, to right the wrong and move forward. We are convicted; we learn and grow. But it is the enemy who condemns us, who makes us feel unforgiven and guilty, and who then works through others to perseverate on condemnation. God wants us to have joy and to see joy. He wants us to see the good in people and to "take the plank out of our own eye" first.

These things have I spoken unto you, that my joy might remain in you, and that your joy might be full.
—John 15:11 (KJV)

I watched my little granddaughter grow up with joy, appreciation, and love. She was strong like her momma. She sometimes ended up with hurt in her heart because she looked at life through a filter of joy and often didn't see the "meanness" of life coming at her. Those rose-colored eyes of hers blocked out the dark rays.

Once, when her momma was about the same age, she came home from school in a complete tizzy. A new little girl had just joined their first grade class; she was partially blind and walked with a guide cane. Well, that cane might as well have been a magic wand, and the little girl might as well have been wearing a princess crown. She was a sweet child and received loads of attention because of her condition. A group of classmate girls formed a whirlpool of whispers and were convinced that she wasn't as blind as she seemed. They felt she was getting all the attention from the teacher and everyone else—needlessly. Our own daughter even said that maybe her blindness wasn't really that bad. We could see that a mountain of jealousy was building in that first-grade class and a dose of empathy was needed—and STAT!

We knew there were many other ways to be blind in life.

When our daughter came home from school the next day, her dad asked her to come out in the backyard. She and her brother often played on a homemade "rocket ship," so she delightfully ran to the backyard. Before she could charge outside he asked her to wait as he wanted to show her something. Carefully, her dad tied a red bandana around her eyes and head, and then he said, "Okay, you can go outside now." He explained that she could see light and had a memory of what was in her own backyard but her new friend couldn't do that. Her friend didn't know her way around school. He told her to walk to the rocket ship and back.

Determined to show how easy that would be, she took off. That stubborn curly headed girl bumped, tripped, and felt her way to the "ship"; she tagged it and made her way back to the screen door. We thought we had bombed on the parenting teaching experience because she made her way there and back so successfully. She stood tall and didn't say a word as her dad untied the bandana. But, as he took it off, big tears flowed down her face. She jumped in his arms. "Daddy, that was so hard. I'm so sorry for my friend." We both hugged her and didn't have to say a word.

That's how Jesus is with us. When we need a lesson, we will be taught what to do; and then He will help us do it and be ready for our arms.

So, how do we stay unblinded?

How do we see life through rose-colored-eyes? Or should we?

For me, it seems, life is a constant learning experience. Sometimes I think I will never achieve the goal. I am constantly having those *Ah-ha!* thoughts and looking backwards or analyzing why I said this or why I did that.

I have learned that frequently my life's heart lessons from God come through a person rather than a priest or a preacher. In fact, when I get those heart lessons, I actually understand the preacher and the Bible better!

One of my best heart lessons was from my younger brother, Steve, who died recently. Sadly, my sister Cathy (#6), found him dead. She had helped him for years.

He was a product of the sixties and carried some of those scars with him his whole life. He studied at a Bible college and spent too much time, we thought, reading and learning the Bible. Absolutely no one knew or could preach, and I

Brother Steve and Anne

mean preach loudly, the Bible like him.

Oh, he wasn't always this way. He loved hard rock, played a mean guitar, could sing like Jim Morrison, and loved to p-a-r-t-y!

My brother also joined the Navy, went to Vietnam, married a neat lady, and had three fine children. But along the way he stumbled and fell to some old "demons," as he would say. He saw them in his shadows, but he also found comfort in the Word of God and would make sure everyone else heard that WORD too—whether they wanted to or not!

He lived a hard life and was helped over and over by many family, medical, and veterans' groups, but it was his Bible that gave him the most comfort. It was not unusual to take him to a department store and have him preach to every single person passing him in and out of the store. I spent a lot of time with him as he aged and, sadly, I confess, for years I was blinded to the courage he actually had and to the information I was being exposed to. Often, my poor brother would crash and have to be picked up on the streets, and I would "listen" to his endless preaching.

He loved to tell me about how:

Nebuchadnezzar came as close as he could to the door of the flaming furnace and shouted: 'Shadrach, Meshach, and Abed-

nego, servants of the Most High God, come out! Come here!'
So Shadrach, Meshach, and Abednego stepped out of the fire.

—Daniel 3: 20–26 (KJV)

On good days he would tell me I was going to survive that fire, but on bad days he would say we would all be burned up. I let it go in one ear and out the other. I never thought that I would ever really go through a fire that could make me stronger or better! He tried to teach me. I loved him, but I was blinded by his condition and didn't see or hear him.

Sometimes, as he aged, when we picked him up we would clean him up, wash his sore, tired, street-walking feet, and get him some food and cool air conditioning. As he preached to me in a coffee shop one day, he looked deep at me with his beautiful blue eyes and said "Jesus loves you, Anne."

Okay, yeah, yeah, Jesus loves me, I thought. He said it again. "Jesus loves you, Anne." I guess it was obvious that I wasn't listening, so he stood up and proclaimed it at the top of his lungs. "JESUS LOVES YOU, ANNE."

My first thought was complete embarrassment in this upscale coffee shop in central Houston.

When pride cometh, then cometh shame: but with the lowly is wisdom

—Proverbs 11:2 (KJV)

Then I saw the man next to me smile sweetly. Another couple walked up to me and the woman put her hand on my shoulder and said "He's right you know!" and she shook hands with my brother. My brother was shining. He whispered, "Thank you, Jesus!" These strangers heard him, they cared about him, they believed him, and they were not embarrassed by his loud words. My eyes were filled with tears. I slumped in my chair and saw my little brother eye to eye for the first time in a long time.

*Bring forth the blind people that have eyes, and the deaf that
have ears.*

—Isaiah 43:8 (KJV)

Finally, "I got it" completely. My brother's journey is our journey—
we are all here to help each other, during all of our different phases
and stages. He was one of my teachers on earth, and he helped me as
much, or more, than I ever helped him.

My brother was just like me—just like all the upwardly mobile
people in the coffee shop. We were all on a journey together, and we
all needed our feet washed at times.
We are all here to receive and share
God's grace. My brother had told me
the truth: Jesus does love me.

My brother unblinded us all in the
coffee shop that day. He was teaching
us about unconditional love with his
sparkling blue eyes that are now fixed
on Jesus in eternity.

Washing feet

When I drive by the homeless, the
tired, the aching, especially the older homeless men, I say "Hello" to
my brother. I don't judge whether they look like scammers, or if they
are smoking cigarettes—sometimes, not always, I give them money,
but I always say a prayer and give a smile. Sometimes, I give them
some water, or a card inviting them to church. I try to look at them
without judgment, with a "there but for the grace of God go I" attitude, and I try to think about how they all had a life once, a mother,
maybe a sister. I remind myself to remember to look at everyone with
kindness, without pre-conceived notions, and I think about Molly,
that long-ago six-year-old, now twenty-three-year-old Texas A & M
graduate granddaughter of mine, when she said "*Mimi, I think I have
rose colored eyes.*"

And I whisper, *Thank you, Jesus!*

Molly Martin, Texas A&M

VIEWPOINT

Definition:

• A mental position from which things are viewed.

• A place from which something can be viewed (Princeton World-Net). Attitude of mind (Random House Dictionary).

> *Let nothing be done through strife or vain glory;*
> *but in lowliness of mind let each esteem other better than them-*
> *selves.*

> —Philippians 2:3 (KJV)

Try a *Happy Jesus Nurse* examination of your viewpoint of life.

IS YOUR VIEWPOINT TRULY HONEST, or is it someone else's vision?

• WHO do you let decide your viewpoints? God or society?

• WHERE are you when viewing life? WHAT place are you in while viewing people? Are you on your "high horse" or in a pit? Are you having a "pity party"? Are you OKAY, but everyone else isn't?

• WHEN did you view a person or life event incorrectly and realize you were wrong? Family of origin? Spouse? Friends? Colleagues?

• WHY did you view the situation in that manner? Is it something in your own heart that needs to be examined?

BLIND SPOT: Blind spots in life are physical, mental, and spiritual. There is an actual biological space where the image that the eye is "seeing" hits the optic disc of the eye and cannot be seen. The image is there but one cannot see it in that particular area.

In psychological terms, a blind spot actually starts as a protective mechanism, a defense, to block something, such as a feeling, behavior, memory, or issue that would be painful to experience or deal with (psychology dictionary).

TIPS:

Most of us experience blind spots in life, and the Holy Spirit can rip the veil off of them—but only when we are ready and prepared to face them!

- First PRAY! Ask the Holy Spirit to come inside you.

- Study the Word of God. Start with Proverbs, and apply the wisdom and discernment to your own life.

- If a persistent viewpoint emerges in your life around your behavior— irritability, envy, sanctimonious behavior, greed, pity, pride, etc.—take note of you. Find a trusted friend who can tell you what they "see." Listen to them!

- If you find yourself frequently attributing certain characteristics to others, they may reflect the viewpoints you hold in your own heart. You may be projecting them on to others (another defense mechanism).

- Keep a three-day journal. Simply jot down two columns: Negative and Positive. Write down the words and statements coming out of your own mouth each day, what you say about situations and direct towards others (traffic, people, work, etc.) Do they belong in the Negative column or the Positive column? Tally them all up, and see which you say the most.

- Try a "Day of Positives," Prepare your house by putting positive notes and scriptures around the house; practice reciting positive statements to otherwise potential negative "triggers" for yourself.

- Think, and then speak positive words out loud so your own brain will hear them and you will begin to rebuild a healthy viewpoint. Dr. Caroline Leaf's book, *Switch on Your Brain*, states that negative thinking "creates atypical responses in the brain which will result in atypical manifestations." (p.88, used with permission of the author).

- Your thinking can and will change your responses, behaviors, and viewpoints on life! Work daily toward PURE heart motives, toward a positive viewpoint and a healthier life.

- At the same time, don't be too hard on yourself!

Blessed are the pure in heart: for they shall see God

—Matthew 5:8 (KJV)

The Beaded Purse
PRIORITIES

✥

And I will give thee the treasures of darkness, and hidden riches of secret places, that thou mayest know that I, the LORD, which call thee by thy name, am the God of Israel.

—Isaiah 45:3 (KJV)

I could only imagine how important the beaded purse was to her, my little, five-foot-tall grandmother who gave me her height. She wore pearls, and she absolutely always had on lipstick, carefully brushed on with a lipstick brush. She was from Los Angeles, and her sister was in the movies. We loved to hear her stories. Her father was in vaudeville, and she knew about many early movie stars—the good, the bad and the ugly.

One time, her sister got her a job as an extra in a Cecil B. DeMille movie. She even had a line to speak and practiced it for days: "What's the matter, dear?" But her claim to fame was not being in the movie but that when she went to the movie set wearing modern-day nail polish and the famous director saw it and yelled at her, she walked off the set and went home!

Granny "Jewel" and Anne

My Granny's name was Julia but she

was called "Jewel"—how perfect! She had dreams of treasures in life and married too early, bringing five children into this world. She smiled a lot and was full of encouragement for her children; my mother was number four. We had moved to the faraway state of Texas, miles from the California clan, but somehow we managed to always stay connected. We craved stories of sunny, futuristic California, and they craved stories of horses, cowboys, and "y'alls" from Texas. Sometimes cousins would phone just to hear us talk funny! So, we always hammed it up and prolonged the drawls.

My grandparents loved to dress up in the day—and I mean dress up. Gramps was a men's clothier at *Desmonds* and knew how to dress—men's topcoat, hat, and suits of the best fabrics. He was also a hot air balloon soldier who survived WWI, "the war to end all wars," but he would never talk about that. They also lived during the WWII blackouts in California. Granny fed "hobos," as she called them, out of the back door during the Depression. They also danced and dined during the big-band era with Benny Goodman himself, as well as partied during the early heyday years of Los Angeles and Hollywood. Every now and then, she could be persuaded to do a little Charleston dance. It. Was. The. Bomb!

Even a vacation trip to Hawaii involved wearing the proper clothes. Especially a hat!

Every week on Sunday my Granny went to Mass. She also worked at the church rectory to get a discount on her children's Catholic school tuition. But on those weekend nights, when a little extra money was available, the sequined dress, the black heels, definitely a feathered hat, and that beaded purse came out.

Grandparents, Jewel and Earl Evans in Hawaii

So, when my cousin Kathy called me two weeks after her mother, my mom's sister Marilynn died, I was curious when she told me she was sending

Granny's beaded purse

me a package. She said it held a few of the most important items she had left from my grandmother. Well, I never expected that I would be the one to receive the beaded purse. I knew how important that was!

The package came and I carefully opened it, setting the other items aside to get to the prize. I unwrapped the purse and instinctively, immediately looked inside. I expected to see her constant feminine handkerchief, lipstick, and maybe a hidden coin or secret cigarette holder! I thought of the times her hands opened and closed the clasps, sometimes nervously, maybe even held it as she twirled around in her dressy dress in front of a mirror or put it on a table by the dance floor as she was swept into the arms of my grandfather. I could only imagine how important the small purse was to her.

I opened the rest of the package and found a zippered case. Oh yes, I forgot. My wise California cousin had said, "I am sending you what was most important to Granny in a zippered case. I want you to have it."

Okay, she meant the beaded purse, right?

I opened the zippered bag and found a feathery paper, fragile, Daily Missal prayer book. The pages opened automatically to places marked

Granny's prayer missal

for years by funeral holy cards for friends and relatives, a Saint Christopher medal, and little torn pieces from other pages that were saved rather than discarded. This treasure had been preserved in a zippered bag and was over sixty-five years old. I was afraid to touch it. It was all taped up and held together. It was obviously vulnerable. I was confused. This woman who lived through some of the most pivotal and exciting times of America's history, who knew movie stars' secrets, who listened to musicians' struggles, and politicians' war stories, valued this prayer book most of all?

I mean, I knew she was religious but I thought it was just a part of her life that she fit in with all the other exciting and glamorous events of her days. I thought it was more about her Irish roots and rituals, not real God stuff.

I looked through the prayer book and saw the old division of English and Latin prayers that I remembered so well as a child. I saw all the prayers for the sick and hopeless, especially prayers to St. Jude, my mom's favorite saint, prayers for families and marriages, prayers during Masses for the many seasons, for people, for the church: Advent, Christmas, Lent, and Easter; prayers for all the sacraments: Baptism, Communion, Confirmation, Extreme Unction (which is what the last rites were called back then), and of course, for funerals.

It was as regular as the tide, the sun, and the moon. It could be counted on when the world, or yourself, was falling apart. It was a constant in the ever-changing times.

I knew my Granny loved her Rosary and her rituals, but I never thought it was actually a first priority in her life. I knew she was always kind and helped other people, but I just thought that was her personality, not her passion or calling. I knew she and my grandfather had a split-religion home where she had won the issue on how to raise the children—he being from the large Evans family of the Salt Lake City Mormons and her from the O'Crowley Irish Catholics. They respected each other's background but then with no disagreement, they went to Mass.

I kept reading through the marked pages wondering why in the world she had flagged the prophecies section, the Genesis and Old Testament stuff. Was she trying to make sense out of life too? Was she scared about the world around her? Was she worried about something in her family or in her home? Did she feel like me sometimes?

Did she pray directly to God, or did she just go to church to meet some longstanding obligation?

Did she talk to Jesus?

And then I saw on the last page of her prayer book, her own handwritten formal prayer, correctly punctuated and all.

It was stunning to see. I felt I had peeked into her heart to read it, starting with its heading of Sept. 14th, 1955. She began with, "O Jesus, true friend of the humble worker, Thou has given us in thy servant "Matthew" a wonderful example of victory over vice, a model of penance and love...."

Oh dear, my cousin was right. My granny's treasure was this prayer book. She had saved it all these years. Her connection to Jesus was her favorite treasure.

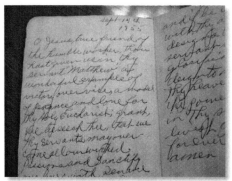
Granny's handwritten prayer, 1955

I was waiting for the beaded purse. I was excited about possessing the treasure of my heart. I had placed the beaded purse above it all. The word penance from her sixty-year-old prayer hit me between the eyes.

I gently swept over the pages of her heartfelt prayer with my fingertips and I prayed also:

O Jesus, true friend of your humble servant, you have given us your examples of what is truly valuable. Help me to put YOU first in my daily walk with life and to appreciate my ancestors, remembering all their prayers that have gone before me. And may they know how much I value them and what is really important. Thank you for my Granny...

...

Oh, and one more thing, if it's okay to say, Jesus, thank you also for her beaded purse that brought her so much joy! Amen. �֎

PRIORITIES

Definition:

• Precedence, especially established by order of importance or urgency (American Heritage Dictionary of English Language, Fourth Edition, updated 2009 by Houghton Mifflin Co.)

• Priorities are what you value most in life.

> *But seek ye first the kingdom of God, and his righteousness; and all these things shall be added unto you.*
>
> —Matthew 6:33 (KJV)

TIPS:

• Healthy Priorities are based on a relationship with GOD first—not material things, or other people, or building your image, or the media, or cultural pressures.

• It's important to identify your SOUL PRIORITIES.

• Once identified, if you are clear on where you stand on what is really important in your life, the less chance you will have of being influenced by societal priorities.

• Knowing your priorities is not about making a list and deciding what you need to do first in a day or in life; that is triage and appropriate when outlining tasks. But SOUL PRIORITIES are knowing who and what you actually put first in your daily life and then peeling away your own layers to find out why.

• Ask the Holy Spirit to guide you; examine your own priorities and values, not what someone else values. What you value will direct you!

• Make a list of your life values, and then give examples of how you actually live your values. For example, if "helping people" is a priority of yours, do you actually "walk the walk"? Do you look at other people through Christ's eyes?

- Write down behaviors and methods that will guide you to bridge your priorities to your actual behavior.

- REMEMBER:

Commit thy works unto the LORD, and thy thoughts shall be established.

—Proverbs 16:3 (KJV)

Sycamore Wind
LIFE STORMS

⋆⋆⋆

What time I am afraid, I will trust in thee.
—Psalm 56:3 (KJV)

I t's just the swish of the wind, I whispered to myself late at night. I loved to hear the wind, however softly, flow through the large paper-like Sycamore leaves in our neighbor's backyard. The tree had fulfilled its prediction and grown almost forty feet so far. The bark was beginning to camouflage; the tree was ready to exfoliate and shed; and its large leaves were beginning to dry out, making ready for some of the only real autumn color in southern

Houston, Texas. I so enjoyed this tree, the way it had a main branch that pointed west—it just seemed adventurous!

The Sycamore loves water and absolutely nothing smells sweeter than a Sycamore tree after a rain. Unbeknownst to this one, it was getting ready to be inundated by torrential rain with the arrival of Hurricane Ike.

The weatherman said it was to be a

Old Sycamore tree

long night. So I put my Bible on the floor

in the hall, next to my flashlight. *You just never know.*

The city "hunkered down," as our county commissioner instructed us to do, and Houstonians did what we do best before hurricanes: We gassed up our cars, got some cash, bought up all the batteries, ice, flashlights, radios, bread, masking tape (for windows, which doesn't work at all); we cooked up (barbequed, if possible) all the freezer meat, stocked up on bread, peanut butter, jelly, and, oh, yes, truth be told, most bought beer too. It's just a silly tradition for described hurricane parties but it can also substitute for medicine on a long scary night. Sibling #2, Karen, was totally ready…she even had some generators!

In a Hurricane warning, the shelves in all the stores go bare and fifty miles away the coast gets ready!

I was afraid of this storm. It was 2008. My father had just died six weeks earlier, and my mother was still in shock. We were very sad too. Even though he was gone, and no longer able to help with taping windows and doors, I remembered the time he did during Hurricane

Beach before storm

Carla back in the 1960s.

Houston trees after storm

It was the pine trees we worried about then. They grew all around our house and were bending and snapping to the hundred-mile-per-hour wind gusts in our neighborhood. The children were all afraid of the pops, cracks, and roars throughout the night, but my mother was more stunned by having nine children at the time and spending two weeks without electricity, ice, or money!

So Houston had experience with storms. The city had been almost decimated in 2001 by a tropical storm bearing the pretty, soft name of Allison. Thankfully, our Houston bayous can take a load of water, but forty inches in a couple of days was Noah-like rain, and we felt every drop.

But this night we prepared for Hurricane Ike—a hard consonant, '50s-type president's named storm. My husband prepared the exterior and I took care of the interior. It was quiet, darkening, with a moistness blowing through the Sycamore tree.

We waited.

Flooded Houston streets

For thou hast been a shelter for me, and a strong tower from the enemy.

—Psalm 61:3 (KJV)

Part of the ritual, preparedness, and comfort during a bad storm is being able to talk to family and friends on the phone, to listen to the weather experts, and to check the radar for exactly where the hurricane was going and how strong it appeared. Knowing someone was watching over the storm, standing with you, and going through the experience was emotionally critical. My husband was good about not worrying, unless something actually happened.

Me, however, I was a worrier and had trust issues! Thus, I usually over prepared. So, after watching the people's suffering from the horrors of flooding during New Orleans' Hurricane Katrina, I made him put an axe, flashlight, raincoats, blankets, and a tarp in our attic—just in case we had to chop our way out of the roof.

I know, I know, just a little over the top!

The sun also ariseth, and the sun goeth down, and hasteth to his place where he arose.[6]

*The wind goeth toward the south, and turneth about unto the
north; it whirleth about continually, and the wind returneth
again according to his circuits.[7]
All the rivers run into the sea; yet the sea is not full; unto the
place from whence the rivers come, thither they return again.*

—Ecclesiastes 1:5–7 (KJV)

I stayed on the phone with my daughter, son and sisters. Storm
adrenaline always pumps up a feeling of anticipation and excitement
during the preparedness phase! They were all safe and tucked in. Our
son lived 200 miles away and was begging us to evacuate to San Anto-
nio. He had an extra bedroom. We felt safe, my husband assured him.
NOT ME! I wanted to scream!

Number six sibling, Cathy, welcomed numerous relatives to her
house for safety only to have sister Julie never get off the floor of her
kitchen pantry, door closed, and on the phone with me! Locked in fear!

We were a mess. It seemed the men were all "doing stuff," and the
women were too…worrying!

Now, in every bad Gulf storm there is always that moment when
the wind begins to roar, the fences shake and crack, the phone starts
to crackle, the transformers explode with purple light, the lights start
to flicker and the television goes out!

ALL ALONE IN THE DARK. Our big beautiful city.

Panic rose up in me. I looked to my husband for safety, and he put
his arm around me saying, "We will be okay, I promise."

I am glad he couldn't
see me and my
doubting face.

Slowly the winds
increased with the
whining roar only a
Hurricane can bring.
It is unlike any other

Houston, Texas syline

sound. I tried to think positive and even biblical. I remembered when I was confirmed at church and we received the seven gifts of the Holy Spirit—wisdom, understanding, counsel, fortitude, knowledge, piety, and fear of the Lord. The Holy Spirit was always described to us as coming like a wind.

> *And when he had said this, he breathed on them, and saith unto them, Receive ye the Holy Ghost.*
> —John 20:22 (KJV)

Well, this wind didn't feel like a gift, and I certainly didn't feel like I had any of the acquired gifts, except for fear of the Lord! I'm pretty sure my husband was faking it too, but I borrowed his persona for a while. Then I got my blanket and pillow and lay down in the hallway with my Bible and flashlight. I knew I needed words stronger than the wind to calm my soul.

> *And they came to him, and awoke him, saying, Master, master, we perish.*
> *Then he arose, and rebuked the wind and the raging of the water: and they ceased, and there was a calm.*
> —Luke 8:24 (KJV)

Oh, Lord, who am I to get in such a tizzy over a storm that will come and go? Who am I to feel alone when I know YOU are there? It's just a storm that will be temporary and inconvenient, and it is part of your designed nature.

Lord, who am I to worry, when there are people on the Gulf Coast who are struggling to live right now, and I am in my tight little home with a strong husband? Please keep those people who are suffering and afraid safe.

Storms evoke the call to trust and to have faith and hope. Storms of life strengthen us all. Their very nature demonstrates our lack of control. We can prepare and be ready for the aftermath, but we can't really control a large tree falling on our roof, or a tornado dropping

from the squall line and blowing through our city, or the rain filling
up our streets and flooding our homes. All we can really do is pray,
trust in God, help others around us to do the same, and then help
each other if bad things happen.

This reality always brings me PEACE. When I "let go and let God,"
I almost always smile. It is just such a great feeling of relief.

The "dark and stormy night" rolled on for hours. For some reason,
at one point our telephone land line connected and rang out, and we
talked to our daughter.

"Are you okay? The kids?"

"Yes, and you?"

"Yes, playing games by flashlights."

"Molly?"

"Yes, she's finding batteries...."

That was it, the phone went dead again. But what a gift to connect
heart to heart and know they were still there.

I thought about the Sycamore tree as I heard the many limbs
falling and hitting the roofs around us. I thought about how old it already was and that it had probably gone through Hurricane Carla and
other storms too. I pictured its paper thin, shedding bark and how it
shredded and peeled like torn paper as it grew from the inside out.
I thought about how adversity had made it stronger, how growth
came from stress.

I tapped into that tree's strength and fell asleep on the floor.

There is no man that hath power over the spirit to retain the
spirit; neither hath he power in the day of death.

—Ecclesiastes 8:8 (KJV)

The next day brought the proverbial aftermath. Trees were down,
houses were broken, island homes were washed away...with people.
Shock was seen in new, young neighbors' faces, curfews were out-
lined—no gas, no ice, little food, and like my momma's storm, no
electricity for two weeks!

As husbands cleared yards, families began to pull together. It was something to behold. Neighbors reached out to each other, just like in the "old days." People checked on each other, met their neighbors, brought food and precious coffee to those who had no lights. You could hear the roar of generators from the truly prepared but, although unsafe, it was more common to see long orange extension

cords strung across streets from homes lucky to have electricity to power up a neighbor for a while, just to help them save their refrigerated food or keep a baby's milk cold

The nights were dark; families put chairs outside and visited in the cooler

John cleans storm damage

air, playing guitars, sharing bread and batteries. It was a true hurricane after-party!

Our grandson Matt was six years old at the time, and he still talks about the storm as an adventure. He loved the sharing and the camp-out type of living. But he also loved hearing about the city coming together to help those less fortunate. Even after the scary storm, our oldest grandson, Casey, fearlessly still lives on Galveston Island and even helped with rebuilding after Ike, just like his great-great-grand-father, Walter E. Stewart, helped build the seawall after the Great Storm of 1900. Grandson Jack, in college, still stays in touch for weather reports whenever storms begin to build, and Molly keeps plenty of batteries.

Their daddy, Larry, automatically buys meat to grill for the neighbors whenever a storm is brewing in the Gulf, and gets his barbeque pit all fired up and ready to go! And our son John, Jr. prepares his guest bedroom…just in case.

We learned the meaning of Genesis 50:20 in its deepest sense from that storm, mean Mr. Hurricane Ike:

But as for you, ye thought evil against me; but God meant it unto good, to bring to pass, as it is this day, to save much people alive.

—Genesis 50:20 (KJV)

In other words, what was meant for your harm will be used for your good!

Well, it's July—hot, midsummer again— hurricane season. It's been six years now, so memories fade. Knowing the Holy Spirit is

Grandson Casey—Galveston Beach

always with me, I have less fear and more faith now.

But, I had to laugh when I heard the noise from my back window tonight. I told myself: It's just the swish of the wind—it's just that old Sycamore wind. ✻

LIFE STORMS

Definition:

• STORM: atmospheric disturbance manifested in strong winds accompanied by rain, snow, or other precipitation, and often thunder and lightning (dictionary.search.yahoo.com).

> *Nothing is more beautiful than the love that has weathered the storms of life.*
>
> *The love of the young for the young, that is the beginning of life, but the love of the old for the old, that is the beginning of things longer.*
>
> —Jerome K. Jerome

> *But we have this treasure in earthen vessels, that the excellency of the power may be of God, and not of us.*
>
> —2 Corinthians 4:7 (KJV)

• Storms can come in all forms and often appear like a thief in the night—a phone call, a diagnosis, a betrayal, an estrangement, a discovery, a lie, a revelation, a confession, a death—even an actual meteorological storm.

• Storms of life are tests, revelations, and building blocks of our inner strength—and yes, often much good can come out of a storm, just like a real storm has rainbows.

• It is in adversity that we meet ourselves and learn or change our character.

> *"And when he was entered into a ship, his disciples followed him.*[24]
>
> *And, behold, there arose a great tempest in the sea, in so much that the ship was covered with the waves: but he was asleep.*[25]

And his disciples came to him, and awoke him, saying, Lord,
   save us: we perish.[26]
And he saith unto them, Why are ye fearful, O ye of little faith?
Then he arose, and rebuked the winds and the sea; and there
was a great calm.[27]
But the men marveled, saying, What manner of man is this,
   that even the winds and the sea obey him!"

           —Matthew 8:23–27 (KJV)

- But it can be so difficult to not be afraid in a storm! (I still work daily on fear.)

- It's all about faith and trust in Jesus (which took me forever to realize).

- But Psalm 50:15 really is the truth—and it works!

   And call upon me in the day of trouble:
   I will deliver thee, and thou shalt glorify me.

           —Psalm 50:15 (KJV)

- Fear and the storm in your life may not be relieved completely, immediately, or even shortly, but sometimes the relief can be in the snap of a finger or it comes in a change or shift in your life—something unimaginable from God. It will reveal to you that GOD IS IN CONTROL.

- It's all God's timing. And sometimes we are left in a stormy period for a while to refine our character.

   And I will bring the third part through the fire, and will refine
     them as silver is refined, and will try them as gold is tried:
     they shall call on my name, and I will hear them:
   I will say, It is my people: and they shall say, The LORD is my
     God.

           —Zechariah 13:9 (KJV)

- REMEMBER: Jesus already delivered us from the biggest storm of all—condemnation and eternal death. So He will be at our side for all other storms of life.

What shall we then say to these things?
If God be for us, who can be against us?

—Romans 8:31 (KJV)

Cleaning Out Closets
RELEASE

✻

For afore the harvest, when the bud is perfect,
and the sour grape is ripening in the flower,
he shall both cut off the sprigs with pruning hooks,
and take away and cut down the branches.

—Isaiah 18:5 (KJV)

"He chopped down my Ligustrum hedges!" screamed our neighbor while pounding on our front door.

"Uh-oh," my mom said before opening the door. She had heard this before. One time it was the corner neighbors' Tallow tree—or "trash" tree, as he called it. Another object was an errant movable clothesline hanging over our fence; and once it was a half-built tree house.

The culprit stood at the kitchen sink with his back to the front door in our early Houston Oak Forest house. He was actually whistling. I would like to say it was a mischievous preteen or a troubled adolescent sibling, but it was my sweet, kind father!

After my mom promised the neighbor that we would replace the bushes and that she would "talk" to my dad, he finally turned around.

"What!" he emphasized with his wide blue eyes.

"There was no light coming through on that side of the house, nothing else could grow, and it was time to cut the blockage down," he claimed.

It was time… There was no light….

✵

So, you see, I come by it naturally. I can cut trees, prune vines, and dig out azaleas whenever I think they need it. I can throw away jars of jelly with two spoonfuls left, and I can toss out magazines and newspapers galore. I hate clutter. But this was different—and I knew it. It was time to clean, and I mean really clean out my closets.

In avoidance mode, I started with the many dresses, sweaters, and shoes in the main closets. I stacked the ones I didn't need or was just tired of on the floor to donate to Goodwill. I bagged up raggedy socks and pajamas, and I weeded through belts and purses—anything to delay the deep boxes in the guest bedroom closet!

But, now, it was time.

Anne's closet

I started with the pop-up plastic box first. The first thing I pulled out was a "back and forth" wordy e-mail from a sibling ten years ago. We were each trying to prove our points. Reading it now, none of it made sense. I could see the hurtful words and our "dug in" points. All I could think was "hurt people, hurt people." I couldn't toss it yet. I set it aside.

The next handful of papers contained e-mail chronicles of a major event in my marriage when my husband and I were apart and we both were in pain. I mean Deep-Dark-Kick-in the-Gut pain. Our words had gone back and forth like a ping-pong game, with each paddle strike getting harder and stronger. These papers were something to hang onto—"just in case." I mean, things are great now, BUT "you just never know!" So, I set it aside.

I pulled out the box that held some of my childhood pictures and found many of me and my nine siblings at various stages and in various situations. Being the oldest of ten, it allowed me to think I was wiser than them sometimes and even thought I was in control-not a good way to be but after all, someone had to do it!

Then the pictures of number five in the family popped out—the brother who was closer to Jesus than any of us, the one who struggled to live a good life, and the one who left us this year—and now we were nine. Oh, this cleaning thing hurts!

The next box held letters and cards from my "sometimes" estranged son. Yuck, this will be no fun.

There were sweet cards about what a great mom I was and what great parents we were. There were letters to his dad telling him, "Thanks" for running the roads with him, and listening to all his stories. There were thank-you cards for buying

Brother Steve

him cars and helping him through tough spots. And there were drawings he had done throughout his life and pictures of him with many friends playing basketball and running track. We had packed them all away to physically separate them from our pained hearts. He will come around someday, but this proves he loved us. Right?

I set that box aside.

Then I delved into the large box that held all the precious notes and cards from our soon-to-turn fifty daughter. I found so many funny, quick drawings and pictures of her, cheering, running, playing basketball, as well as personal cards from her incredible four children, our grandchildren. I found a funny craft she had made mixing up the saying from a famous movie with the stitched words: "Love means never saying you're sorry!"

I found the little sweater I had knitted for her and her doll, "Mrs. Beasley," and I found her little scraped white shoes that foretold how

Daughter, Missy, age 6

small her feet would be compared to mine. Oh, this is definite proof that I am loved!

I set this box carefully aside—a keeper for sure!

I sat on the floor like my "Mrs. Annie Marie" doll and looked at the  boxes and stacks of papers around me. *I'm not doing very well in the closet cleaning business!* I thought.

Have you ever examined why you may have trouble letting go of something or someone? Well, I was doing just that. Why do I feel the need to keep the papers to prove I was right? Or the papers to prove I was loved? Or the papers to prove I was hurt?

> *Remember ye not the former things, neither consider the things of old.*
> —Isaiah 43:18 (KJV)

And then I found the box with the notes and cards from my parents and my husband's parents. So many nice thoughts, so many honored memories! In the bottom of the box was a fairly recent picture. I looked closely and could see the photo of my father standing in front of the old house. I felt I could even see the long ago, too-tall, too-dark Ligustrum bushes! I swear my dad had a gleam in his eyes!

I heard God speak to me deep in my spirit. BE GRATEFUL, open your hands and be GIVING. Release Is About Forgiveness! Letting go is about forgiveness and mercy.

Dad at old house

I don't have to keep proof that I was loved—or that I was right. I don't have to keep proof of what someone said or did. God knows it all anyway, and you know what, each of us knows our own truths too. I don't need to prepare for life in courtroom mode for anything. I don't need to get people back with my words or hang on to hurtful stuff. I need to move forward and release…let it go.

Jesus is my counselor. He is always with me.

I do need to forgive and show mercy whenever possible, even with the old stuff in my closets. I pray for a greater ability to let go of hurts and ways to retaliate or how to get even. I pray to be able to sweep my mind of the memories of hurtful words or painful *heart lessons.*

> *For if ye forgive men their trespasses, your heavenly Father will also forgive you:*
> —Matthew 6:14 (KJV)

So, I looked again at the picture of my earthly father standing by the imagined Ligustrum bushes. It was time. *Let in the light!* And I started releasing, tossing, and shredding, opening my clasped, gripped hands, letting go and forgiving! ⚜

RELEASE

Definition:

- To set free from confinement or bondage (verb)
- Relief from suffering (noun)…(Dictionary.search.yahoo.com)

This then is the message which we have heard of him, and declare unto you, that God is light, and in him is no darkness at all.
—1 John 1:5 (KJV)

How do we let go and let in the light of Christ?
How do we release, let go, and forgive hurts or evidence of hurts?
How do we do what is right instead of trying to be right?
I have found out, (the ever-so-hard way), that to Let Go is to give away my perceived right to punish and then to decide to open and release the grip that person has on my own heart.

Forgiveness does not mean you will forget or condone a person's bad choice or behavior, but it means you will RELEASE self-righteousness and vengeance, and thus value them as a person. It is not easy because "triggers" or reminders may pop up and allow bad memories or feelings to surface. Sometimes, friends or family will specifically ask you about certain situations causing the event to resurface. Sometimes television programs or movies will remind you of a painful situation and will model an unforgiving or vengeance-filled type of response causing you to doubt your own forgiving process. This is a character test for you and the enemy's way of tempting you to stay in unforgiveness.

A great reminder: *"Love is an act of constant forgiveness."*

A FIVE-STEP *HAPPY JESUS NURSE* PROCESS OF RELEASE:

(Release begins in your Spirit and by asking Jesus—and it may need to be repeated numerous times!)

1) BEGIN BY ASKING THE *HOLY SPIRIT* TO HELP, and then

agree with yourself to just start the process.

2) START WITH ONE HURT OR ONE INSTANCE and move through the layers, if needed. Remember: You aren't responsible for fixing the person who hurt you, only for forgiving them.

Cast thy burden upon the LORD, and he shall sustain thee: he shall never suffer the righteous to be moved.
                                        —Psalm 55:22 (KJV)

3) SAY *OUT LOUD* TO YOURSELF OR TO A TRUSTED PERSON OR WRITE IT DOWN: Lord, thank you for helping me!

Now, I Release (name) _____

For _____ (be specific)

And I Give (name) _____to You, Jesus.

Please heal my heart of any pain, anger, or desire for revenge.

4) START IMMEDIATELY TO *LET GO AND LET GOD*. Every time the thought about the hurt comes into your mind, replace it, and say, "Jesus is Lord."

5) REMIND YOURSELF: We all need forgiveness. Thank God for forgiving you! Give yourself peace.

If it be possible, as much as lieth in you, live peaceably with all men.
                                        —Romans 12:18 (KJV)

In His Hands
GRIEF/LOSS

᠅

*Wherefore I put thee in remembrance that thou stir up the gift
of God, which is in thee by the putting on of my hands.*

—2 Timothy 1:6 (KJV)

"He's dead," brother Walter (#4) said. He had been with him
all night. His words bounced around in my head like a
pinball, bouncing all the way to pierce my heart. I knew
he was close to the end. I also knew he was ready to go.
He had smiled at us a few weeks earlier and said, "It is time."

But Oh, my soul! How does a child, even a very grown child, let
go of her father? All I could do when I got to his bedside was hold his
hands. They were still warm. They still felt strong and muscled. But
that was it, they were just so still. I held them, and all I could say was
"Thank You. Thank You."

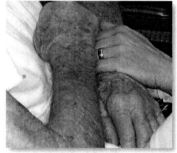
Anne holds father's hands

My father's hands represented so
much to me. They had patted my back,
stirred large pots of chili, driven me to
school, popped firecrackers, opened
doors, crushed empty beer cans, repaired water pumps around the world,
put on butterfly stitches, punched out
neighborhood drug dealers. He was a

champion boxer in the Navy. He taught all ten
of his children to box, as well as in-laws, grandchildren, and neighbors—sometimes with a big
"ouch" to the punch to make sure we remembered to either duck or cover.

My father and I had many deep philo-
sophical and spiritual discussions. I knew well
that his heart was a muscle of peace, love, and
understanding. He had told me many times the
importance of living one day at a time, but he

*Emmett V. Stewart, U.S.
Navy boxer*

showed me late in life how to do just that with him during his last
long days of lost memories on this earth.

He slapped my face with one hand once. I deserved it. I was thirteen years old and had scared
him to death by not coming home on time. It
was getting dark. I disrespected him, and he
was so scared, he cried. As a parent, I know
now how he felt. His hands had held babies and
my mom's arms as they danced in the kitchen;
his hands tore down walls, necessarily, when a
new baby was born; they gestured wildly during
political discussions; they crushed fingers in the

*Anne and father on
horse, San Diego Ranch*

most manly of all handshakes; and they prayed every night over each
of his children as he pointed them to heaven for God's protection.

I Needed My Father's Hands!

I felt so very alone with the finality of my father's breath. Have you
ever looked around for backup in a difficult situation or scary time
and felt all alone? How do children make it in this world without
fathers? Even those not in a family unit are important fathers, and
they will be linked to children forever. Fathers are rocks; they make a
difference.

Even as an adult, I felt my protector, my backup, was now missing.
Then my husband put his hand on my back and I felt his comfort. He

whispered, "Think about his last words." I really couldn't think about anything at that time, and frankly, I didn't want to.

But then it came to me. I remembered days earlier when my father was struggling mightily and my mother was helping him. It was more than his last days in the natural world—it was a *fight* with the hereafter. Those of us who were there just watched in amazement.

My father was pushing his arms and hands, actually "punching" the air and asking my mom to "sweep" away something bad that he saw in front of him. She would push it away and he would frown and say "No, push more." So she would. She pushed away, and then he would point, "No, no, over there," and she would push that side away. And finally, the struggle shifted and he said "Yes, there he is." He completely slumped in his bed and relaxed his shoulders with a peaceful look in his eyes, a look of love on his face. He stared at my mom then and mouthed "I Love You."

It was a bridging gift to us all. We witnessed him begin his transition, and it gave us great comfort. I knew <u>that at death</u> God often sent angels, dead family members, and allowed other spiritual visits in the natural. I had seen glimpses of this as a nurse when patients were dying. We had watched my mother-in-law Maxine's face relax and actually briefly turn into the face of her own mother, at the time of her death. The family around her was amazed as they felt their sweet little grandmother, Mulla, had come to gently take their mother to heaven.

I knew about the spiritual world sometimes permeating the natural world and as a child was told a miracle story by my fathers' mother. She was my brave Irish grandmother who had come to America for a better life at age 14, crowded in the bottom of a boat with many other Irish Immigrants. She often told us of the time when a vision from *Mother Mary* had saved her family from a raging flood in southern California. The valley families were escaping a raging flood in the early 1900s, they were all going in one direction, but my grandmother, Mary Catherine O'Gallagher, knew Mother Mary well, and she saw the *Blessed Mother* calling them in another direction. The real miracle was that she was able to convince my stubborn grandfather to follow her vision, which saved them all.

But my dad's connection with the hereafter was so concrete, so physical, so real, and right in front of us in real time. No angel harps, no floods, no flashing lights. My strong father had boxed with the devil and won. It was his one last fight. He was going home to be in the hands of Jesus.

I saw his earthly hands go away covered with my tears, but I could never have imagined that his hands would guide me again in some stormy months to come. I did not realize that my father's hands would soon be protectively around me during dark nights and would lift me from emotionally painful pits before me.

Mostly, I know now, that Jesus' hands will always be with me, as they will be with you in any time of struggle. Just reach out. They will hold you up, pat your back, open doors, help you stir chili, push you towards good, pull you from harm, and even help you crush beer cans, if needed, in a different kind of way!

His hands will break every chain, fight your battles, defend you from harm, and you will win the fights because...*HE is alive!*

And Israel said unto Joseph, Behold, I die: but God shall be with you, and bring you again unto the land of your fathers.
—Genesis 48:21 (KJV)

GRIEF/LOSS

Definition:

- GRIEF: Deep mental anguish, as that arising from bereavement.
- LOSS: The condition of being deprived or bereaved of someone or something (dictionary.search.yahoo.com)

> *For in much wisdom is much grief:*
> *and he that increaseth knowledge increaseth sorrow.*
> —Ecclesiastes 1:18 (KJV)

- GRIEF HURTS: It hurts physically, mentally, spiritually. Grief and loss can also exacerbate an existing illness, lower the immune system and make us more susceptible to major health problems. Stress reactions described in early research clearly note that in the alarm phase of grief, the immediate pain or event, can cause the sympathetic nervous system in the body to respond with catecholamine hormones like adrenaline. Chemicals are triggered in the brain and body by the hypothalamus to the pituitary gland and then the adrenal glands, which produce ACTH (adrenocorticotrophin hormone). ACTH is the "protection for battle" hormone—it causes the reaction in the adrenal glands to produce cortisol. Initially this hormone is positive, it helps us to be prepared for "fight or flight". But when stress or grief continues over time, chronic high levels of this stress hormone can remain in the blood stream; possibly affecting the immune system. Excessive cortisol is linked to chronic inflammation, damaged blood vessels and brain cells and increased risk for weight gain, colds, sleep deprivation (which also is related to memory loss), depression, ulcers, and joint problems. Unresolved grief and stress may also lead to increased alcohol or drug use, and other unhealthy behaviors. (*AARP Bulletin,*November 2014, *STRESS* by Elizabeth Agnvall; Mary Neis & Melanie McEwen, "Community Public

Health Nursing", 2011; *Cortisol and Stress: How to Stay Healthy*, by Elizabeth Scott, 2014)

If you doubt that stress can seriously affect the body, recognize this fact: Extreme stress, grief, shock, or fear can cause a syndrome known as the "broken heart syndrome," clinically called Takotsubo Cardiomyopathy. With this syndrome, the heart literally changes shape; it morphs and balloons, causing the pumping chambers to have difficulty pumping. The shape change looks like the name of the syndrome (in Japanese the takot subo is an octopus pot) which is similar to the shape the heart takes on with this syndrome. In fact, this shape, with symptoms, is how the syndrome is diagnosed in a cardiac scan. This syndrome is temporary, but it needs to be diagnosed and treated as it can actually be a critical heart condition leading to heart failure. It can be triggered by extremely stressful incidents (emotional and/or physical), and the symptoms mimic a heart attack (myocardial infarction) with chest pain, shortness of breath, and interruption of the heart's pumping and rhythm. It is in reaction to the massive volume of stress hormones and occurs most often in women. (http://www.health.harvard.edu/newsletters/Harvard_womens_health_watch)

- Just think about the old phrase "scared to death" when you think about stress, grief, and loss, and how God designed the body to be on guard and to react to emotions, difficult situations, and danger. Then reverse that in your mind and logic should tell you that if it can go one way (to the negative) it can go the other (toward the positive).

- God will work with you and heal the grief and loss you go through, step by step. It's your choice. You can stay stuck in different phases, or you can work through them. The operative word is "through."

- Grief is like an infection or a "boil" in the body; it must be cleaned out, expressed, and healed with medicine. Otherwise, it can spread and destroy the body, mind, and spirit. God is the main medicine

for grief and loss!
- Let your tears flow—tears kept inside will crack the heart—express them, let them flow; they are filled with healing salve and will water your soul.

Blessed are they that mourn: for they shall be comforted.

—Matthew 5:4 (KJV)

The grief process is not linear. It does have defined phases, but phases that are individual and permeable—they are different for everyone, and there is no "right" or "wrong" way to grieve. When we have a major life issue (health, family, marriage, divorce, crime, death) and thus feel grief, loss, fear, betrayal—major changes in life— we go up and down and in and out of the phases of grief and loss. Grief issues can affect every aspect of our life and often throw us into an incomprehensible vortex of feelings.

The main question is: Are you mostly moving forward? Elizabeth Harper Neeld, PhD, developed one of the most thorough "Models of the Active Grieving Process" in her book, *Seven Choices: Finding Daylight After Loss Shatters Your World.* In the book, she shares her personal experiences with grief and loss as well as her academic knowledge of the topic. Her book describes the choices we can make to move forward after a major life event and how to avoid becoming a "victim" or being stuck in the pain of grief. Dr. Neeld provides a road map that gives us guiding benchmarks for any type of grief. www. elizabethharperneeld.com (See graphic used by permission of the author.)

Working through grief and loss can bring anyone to their knees but it can also allow a more comprehensive understanding of life and help us to empathize with others who are dealing with losses. A magnificent example of this is found in the book "Grace Poured Out"(2014) by Valerie M. Herndon. Her book intimately describes the pain as well as the deepened spiritual strength she and her husband Wes experienced when suffering the immeasurable loss of their daughter Katie. Little Miss Katie was only 15 years old. Her book clearly demonstrates the stages of grief, the anguish of sibling loss on their other children, big brother and sister Nick and Bethany, as well as the rock of Jesus they all held onto that helped them survive. Her book will bless you! http://www.gracepouredout.com/ (used with permission of author)

We know that support from others is also critical when dealing with painful losses. This was seen clearly by those patients working through the early days of the HIV/AIDS crisis. Our community learned much about surviving grief from their actions. (KUHT-TV PBS Production, *Living With AIDS*, 1991, written and produced by Anne Stewart Helton, RN, BSN, MS, and Robert S. Cozens, Houston, Texas, and National PBS)

- Prayer, friends, counselors, support groups, ministers, priests can help you, especially people who have been through what you are experiencing, whatever your circumstance. But your biggest loss would be if you were to deprive yourself from God, from Jesus' healing touch in your life.

- The George Jones song, "Lonesome Valley," is wonderful, but remember: Jesus is with us 24/7; he will walk any lonesome, dark valley with us, we are not alone.

> *The LORD is my shepherd; I shall not want.[2]*
> *He maketh me to lie down in green pastures:*
> *He leadeth me beside the still waters.[3]*
> *He restoreth my soul:*
> *He leadeth me in the paths of righteousness for his name's sake.[4]*
> *Yea, though I walk through the valley of the shadow of death,*
> *I will fear no evil: for thou art with me;*
> *Thy rod and thy staff they comfort me.*
>
> —Psalm 23:1–4 (KJV)

ACTIVE GRIEVING PROCESS MODEL

Elizabeth Harper Neeld, Ph.D. *Seven Choices: Finding Daylight After Loss Shatters Your World.* www.elizabethharperneeld.com (Used by permission of the author.)

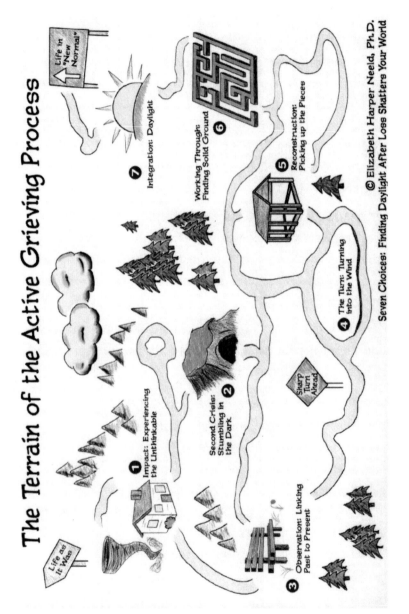

1 **Impact: Experiencing the Loss**
Positive choice: To Experience and Express My Grief Fully
What's normal? Strong emotion; Inability to concentrate; Biorhythms disturbed (sleep, eating, etc.); Anger, guilt, shame; Fear, confusion disorientation; Worry; Situation always on my mind
What helps? Cut ourself slack; Decide what you need; Talk to someone or be with someone who has no agenda except to listen; Find ways to express emotions; Talk to a professional

2 **Second Crisis: Stumbling in the Dark**
Positive choice: To Endure with Patience
What's normal? Loss of "assumptive world"; Feelings of emptiness, helplessness, and hopelessness; Sadness; Decline in health; increase in accidents; Questioning
What helps: Write Take walks, Garden; Get medical checkup; Pray; Slow down; Talk to professional; Wait

3 **Observation: Linking Past to Present**
Positive choice: To Review Honestly
What's normal? Reminiscing; Reviewing positive and negative; Realizing what is hindering; Spending more time alone.
What helps? Consider what gave meaning in the past and how to bring that into the present in new form; Relive events of the past through pictures, writing, scrapbooks, etc.; Review what you are doing when you feel worse and when you feel better; Spend time alone.

4 **The Turn: Turing Into the Wind**
Positive choice: To Replan One's Life
What's normal? Gaining an awareness that our responses to the trransition will determine how we enjoy life; Becoming willing to stop focusing on the past.

What helps? Asserting that you will be responsible for creating a life appropriate to the person you are now and the situation in which you find yourself now,.

5 **Reconstruction: Picking Up the Pieces**
Positive choice: To Take New Actions
What's normal? Beginning to make changes that are hard but beneficial; Developing new skills; Setting new priorities
What helps: Work with a career counselor, a life coach or a group of individuals who are committed to making life-enhancing changes; Talk to someone about any emotional pain, sadness, fear, and sense of helplessness that might recur as you begin to construct a new future; Learn new things; Step out.

6 **Working Through: Finding Solid Ground**
Positive choice: To Engage in New Conflicts
What's normal? Practicing new roles; Dealing with breakdowns and finding creative solutions
What helps? Distinguish problems related to the loss from those that are just part of living; Replenish yourself; Be patient

7 **Integration: Daylight**
Positive choice: To Make and Remake Choices
What's normal? Feeling released; Having a clearer sense of what we believe in and what truths we choose to live by; Looking up and being able to see a horizon; Experiencing a "new normal"
What to do? Celebrate your hard work; Share your wisdom with others; Honor your sense of humor; Keep some time for stillness

visit www.elizabethharperneeld.com

Elizabeth Harper Neeld, Ph.D.   Seven Choices: Finding Daylight After Loss Shatters Your World

Choice Words
FORGIVENESS, MERCY, AND GRACE

✢

And he called the multitude, and said unto them,
Hear, and understand:[11]
Not that which goeth into the mouth defileth a man;
but that which cometh out of the mouth, this defileth a man.

—Matthew 15:10–11 (KJV)

"He said WHAT?" I said. "But that's not true!" My eyes, mouth, and hands were wide open. I may have had tears. "Why are you so upset? It's just a fiction book," she said. "Yes, but full of anger and hate," I said. Have you ever had someone distort situations? Someone you love? Let me tell you, it's a deep-in-the-bones kind of hurt. My relative wanted to be sure I had read what my son had written—not to hurt me, she said, patting my hands, but just to be sure I was prepared for the words to come.

Okay, well that went really well in her mind, I guess. But her words sent me spiraling backwards in time, and I don't think I heard much else from the smiling mouth that was talking to me after that. My initial reaction was to investigate more, to get the exact quotes, and then to get to work disputing them and proving my position—immediately.

Oh my, the power of words!

Shakespeare used all this word pain stuff in Hamlet, but even Thomas Jefferson sent a letter to Thomas Paine in 1796, in which he wrote: "Go on doing with your pen what in other times was done with the sword." And Trace Adkins even said in his country song, you don't talk bad about mama "'Cause them there's fightin' words." So, how could my own son write hurtful words about a fictionalized family? How could he take pieces of truth and twist them under the guise of dark, fictional humor? He was a happy, sweet boy. Words are black and white, they are out there, exposed, they tell a story. They become history or "her story," whichever. They can have life—*If You Let Them!*

Oh yes, and people do let them. Words grow, they spread, they exaggerate through gossip, they have roots; and words can permeate and break hearts. But after all, didn't we all know what is written about words? I confess I didn't pay any attention.

Let no corrupt communication proceed out of your mouth,
but that which is good to the use of edifying,
that it may minister grace unto the hearers.

—Ephesians 4:29 (KJV)

My son's written words go back—they must go way back. Right? In fact, his last book told us things we never knew he was involved in; so it must be our fault!? But as parents, we never heard these words from our daughter, so it doesn't make sense! But sense isn't part of the equation when someone is using painful words. We all see our memories through our own prisms and it takes courage and the Holy Spirit to bypass those prisms and look at ourselves in the mirror. Even Michael Jackson told us that! It's hard to admit, but I have found it's usually because of my own stuffed feelings, internal issues or projections when I have written or said hurtful words. Sometimes I feel I should keep 'duct tape' stored in my purse for my mouth or remove my keyboard when I am feeling upset.! It's difficult to hold back words of hurt, anger, disappointment, or retaliation. And I have definitely used words as weapons myself.

So sorry to all—please forgive me!

⁂

I also knew personally how badly words could hurt and brand people. I was a teenage mother over fifty years ago, and I decided to go forward with my baby inside me. Actually, the word *decided* gives me way too much credit. I never really felt I had any other option. It wasn't because I felt forced, it was because I remember feeling "happy." I loved my boyfriend John (Bob). He was happy too, and we talked of marriage, so that was the next logical step for us, get married—*quickly*—and have our baby. So what if we were in high school! It was everyone else around us who were scurrying around with their hair on fire.

In 1962 there were no easy-access birth control ads, no home pregnancy tests, no high profile media single moms and abortion wasn't considered by us. Few grandparents were raising grandchildren, and there were no schools with day care for teen moms. Besides, I was a Catholic girl, and at that time only "bad girls" were thought to use birth control or know much about sex. Fifty years ago teen pregnancy meant mostly shame, secrets, and hiding. But believe

Anne, pregnant teen

me, (denial served me well) I actually felt joy when the first bumps of life from my son kicked me from inside.

So, as teen parents, we believed in our new charge, and our desire was to start on our journey to raise our son, and soon after that our pretty daughter. Our wedding was simple, private, and scary—and I was sick. Oh my, was I sick with morning sickness!

I threw up daily and was hospitalized several times; and I learned the trials of what mothers everywhere at every age feel. It is a tough road, and I had many people tell me it was my punishment to bear, which

I believed for a long time. It was confusing trying to play grown up, which laid the foundation for doing many things wrong. We didn't know it at the time.

We worked hard to have a good family, and mostly we were just trying to survive and move forward. We put each other through school with menial jobs. My poor hubby, John, always had a 2:00 a.m. paper route; he loaded trucks and pulled the line at the freight lines; he sold fuller brush (for a week); he ground steel, made plumbing line ditches, and scraped rubber in a pit that could kill you. He wouldn't complain or leave any job until he had another because he knew he had to support his family. He was only eighteen years old.

John, Bobby and Missy - 1964

Often, he would come home to clean up from some horrible job before going to night school, and he would turn the water black soaking in the tub while reading his homework for some night class—all while eating food I had fixed him and placed on a tray. Many times, he fell asleep in the tub. Once, I made some hot coffee for him and decided to wake him up with the rich aroma to his nose from the cup of coffee while he was soaking in the tub. It startled him totally. He jumped, and the hot coffee went all over his face. Well, that did wake him up!

Usually, he only had a few minutes between jobs and school. I guess you would say now that we were uber-responsible people. When I hear today about men leaving young pregnant girlfriends to fend for themselves or about sixteen-year-old parents dropping off babies at fire stations or on doorsteps, it sounds like a Dickens tale of long ago. Sometimes, I can remember those obvious feelings of desperation, but we were different.

Or we thought we were.

I would make special foods for my teenage husband and the children, even when we had no money. Cream of wheat was a daily special, with water not milk, but I would always sprinkle cinnamon on it—it was pretty good!

I remember once making popcorn and dripping some vanilla extract on it, to make him a treat. He loved it, and I loved him! We were too proud to ask for help, but sometimes, thankfully, our parents or his responsible big brother, Bill, left bags of groceries on the doorstep of our very humble rented Houston Heights home. We secretly appreciated it.

Sometimes, when we turned the lights on in our old kitchen we

"Little Bobby" and John

had to chase roaches away, but we took turns doing it until we could pay for the exterminator to come out. Oh, and we had little gas stoves to heat our bedrooms, and we put pans of water on top of them because we heard that was safer for the children. It was supposed to add moisture to the room. I guess it worked because they breathed easy at night.

I would always try to have the children fed and ready to play with their daddy, even if only for a few minutes, no matter what time he came home. He loved being around them and would often take them on his paper routes just to be with them.

Every job for him was a stepping stone to another one—to a better life for his family. The jobs came and went. The children started school and so did we.

I always said I lived my life backwards. When he started college, I will never forget the night he came home and said, "You have to do this. You have to go to college." He was like that, always encouraging me and others. So I worked part time and went to the University of Texas, determined to become a registered nurse, and I did, getting a bachelor's degree and then a master's degree from Texas Woman's University.

We will show you world. WE WILL MAKE IT!

We followed all the usual parenting role traps: cub scouts and brownies, mandatory little league, basketball camps at the YMCA, reading books, dance, music, and art classes, and as our income increased, we went to movies, the theater, and short vacations.

Anne graduates, TWU, 1985

The challenge, having started out so young, was that we still had to grow up too. We wanted it all and wanted it fast. We made and lost lots of money. We took many fun trips and had loads of loving times!

Regrets? All parents have some. We spent a major amount of time on our own work and school and our desire to move forward—literally moving too many times to different houses and neighborhoods in order to move up in the world and make a profit. For our children it may have been like pulling blooming tomato plants up by the roots and expecting them to continue blooming when replanted. They had to start over a lot, and they learned to adapt and grow, but it may have scarred them at their roots, their core.

I've heard it said that we live our lives forward but we understand them looking backwards. This is so very true about my experiences. But even Lewis Carroll said, "I can't go back to yesterday because I was a different person then."

Our home always had other family and friends around, especially my nine siblings. They were always in need of something, it was hard but we would have fun when we were all together. Actually, everyone loved to be at our house because we did have fun!

But starting off so early in life was difficult for us both, and we rarely talked about it. We wouldn't ever admit we needed help. Instead, like many parents, sometimes we expressed our frustrations with arguing or stifling feelings, followed by explanations and apologies to each other, and to our children, if needed. Those events were few; they were not physical but they must have been planted and then grew in our son's memories. Now, many of my son's written fiction story words distort the intention and context of family life, but they are his words. We really did the best we could, and we felt we were good parents! I have talked to many other parents who feel discarded by a grown child and I have learned from them to pray, have faith and remain steadfast, remembering Joshua 24:15…"*but as for me and my house, we will serve the Lord*".

So, I have given my son to the Son and I pray that HE softens his heart. After all, I believe, he is HIS son anyway! And, of course,…I. WILL. BE. WAITING. WITH LOVE…

John and Anne, Bobby's Baptism

As the storms deepened in my life, my husband and I continued to busily focus on advancing and surviving. We clearly had neglected to put God first and to deal with our own issues honestly. We failed to nurture our marriage and it cost us dearly. But, "*in nomine Patris, et Filii, et Spiritu Sancti*", (that's Latin folks for "In the name of the Father, the Son and the Holy Spirit"), the saddest thing in the world for me, for us, was that after our children were grown, through with college and on their own life journeys, my husband finally faced some tortuous internal issues and our high-school, sweetheart marriage fell apart. It sure took a long time though; we had been married forty-seven years.

Even with our children being grown up, our split blew up their lives also. All the pain, dirt, scum, spite, scandal, and gossip was spewed everywhere. It was like being in a hurricane during an earthquake, with no weatherman or FEMA director around to help. We were such a mess, and everybody around us knew it. Many, many people tried to help us, but some piled on too. It is amazing what people will say when in a juicy gossip mode. Some difficult-to-forget, hurtful words were said to me and, as people often do, sides were drawn. Sadly, I helped to draw them.

"I never liked him anyway," some relatives said to me. Or "she was always controlling," others chimed in to John. It was that WORD-SWORD thing all over the place. Due to the breakup issues, I had many people on "my side," but John was placed on an island. So many of the people John had helped over his whole life pulled away from him. Some he had bailed out of jail, unbeknownst to their own family; some he had gone to help in the middle of the night for physical or emotional pain or obsessions; or listened to on the phone for hours when they were depressed or suicidal; several he had driven cars home for because they were too drunk to drive; some who had wrecked a car and needed a tow or needed to be picked up from being towed; some who needed a houseful of furniture moved, walls painted, plumbing unstopped, dogs found, hot checks covered, temporary jobs during hard times, small and big loans for every life event imaginable (most never repaid), children in crisis; some even called John in need of having drug dealers confronted or to be driven across country to rehab...John would be there at the drop of a hat.

I saw John helping, but mostly I saw how he didn't reveal the "ugly" side of what the person was going through. He defended them. He always said he didn't believe in "kicking someone when they were down," and he wasn't raised with gossipy behaviors, but now no one defended him.

Here he was being kicked and gossiped about. But I confess, I wanted him kicked at the time too for hurting me. My major character flaw during this time was getting even. I allowed myself to be around what I term the "dark watchers." These are people who enjoy the drama, pain, negative action, and gossip of someone in trouble or in a bad place. Then, when they "get the dark dirt," they usually disappear. Sadly, at times, I defaulted to this dark place. I felt that revenge wasn't always a meal best served cold. I wanted it immediately but then there was that whole Leviticus and Romans thing!

Thou shalt not avenge,
nor bear any grudge against the children of thy people,
but thou shalt love thy neighbour as thyself:
I am the LORD.

—Leviticus 19:18 (KJV)

Dearly beloved, avenge not yourselves,
but rather give place unto wrath: for it is written,
Vengeance is mine; I will repay, saith the Lord.

—Romans 12:19 (KJV)

After forty-seven years, we had scores of family and friends in our lives, and no one could believe we broke apart—especially our grown-up kids. We all hurt. This *heart lesson* was a heart attack. Through the pain, the anger, the loneliness, our scarred-over teenage hearts finally let out all the stored-up, hidden-with-pride, tears and fears.

But, eventually, alone, deep in our own individual life storm, flat on the floor, we each realized what was totally missing from our lives and from our parenting—after all these years. But, it took some kind of *Holy Spirit* blowing down upon us before we reached up to JESUS with our confessions.

"My Refuge and Salvation"
original artwork by Baron
and Barbara Bissett (used by
permission)

I DON'T KNOW!

"Oh, my God, I am heartily sorry for having offended thee. . ."

We needed to surrender and say the REAL CHOICE WORDS: *Oh God! Oh Jesus! Okay!*

It all happened in the most miraculous way, but then God is like that. So, what does all of this have to do with my son's words about a fictionalized me? His family? His take on family life?

Actually, maybe nothing! But then that's the point...I don't have to know...God does.

But as a mother, I guess, I always think everything was my fault with my children, or it's my unhealthy way of staying connected to them, or believing I have control—I'm working on that. I know I can't control or change anyone and everyone makes their own choices..

For now we see through a glass, darkly; but then face to face:
now I know in part; but then shall I know even as also I am known.

—1 Corinthians 13:12 (KJV)

I have to look in my own mirror, *Mrs. Annie Marie*, but somehow my own story seems to be part of the whole story. It's my son's desire to sort it all out, and his words are his choice; he has his own consequences too. I have to let it go and stay vigilant with my own written and spoken words.

Death and life are in the power of the tongue:
and they that love it shall eat the fruit thereof.

—Proverbs 18:21 (KJV)

I have learned that Jesus was so very careful about what He said when He walked the earth. Not only did Jesus choose his words wisely, but he chose when to even speak or respond. Others wrote His words. Others wrote His story.

Who, when he was reviled, reviled not again;
when he suffered, he threatened not;
but committed himself to him that judgeth righteously.

—1 Peter 2:23 (KJV)

What a timeless message He modeled for us. His enemies were always trying to trap him with words, with questions, and he would thoughtfully turn their words right back to them, or He would answer minimally.

He heard the lies, the misinterpretations of His intentions and lessons. He could see straight to the hearts of anyone speaking against Him, and he didn't waste time arguing or trying to win a word battle. Instead, He always pushed forward doing His Father's work, helping and healing with LOVE.

Often, it's the words of battle that become cemented into our hearts and minds and then lead to words of revenge. And then those words can lead toward the unending cycle to WIN, and it spirals out of control. It becomes a tug of war. Sometimes, even well-meaning people will drop us in life. Sometimes, it has nothing to do with us; they are dealing with their own issues. But I now know that there will always be a Simon to help me carry my cross too, even if I let slip words of anger, revenge, and hurt.

> *And as they came out, they found a man of Cyrene,*
> *Simon by name:*
> *him they compelled to bear his cross.*
>
> —Matthew 27:32 (KJV)

So the next time someone tells me what my son said or wrote, I may think, "He said what? But that's not true," and feel the hair rise up and tingle on my Irish fighting arms. But then I will try to remember:

> *She openeth her mouth with wisdom;*
> *and in her tongue is the law of kindness.*[27]
> *She looketh well to the ways of her household,*
> *and eateth not the bread of idleness.*
> *Her children arise up, and call her blessed;*

her husband also, and he praiseth her.

—Proverbs 31:26–28 (KJV)

Ahhh, and then I pray that I will remember the butterfly feelings of joy from the little kicks inside my sixteen-year-old tummy and choose to say about and to my son, even if in correction, only ***choice words*** based on love. ✤

FORGIVENESS, MERCY, AND GRACE

Definition:

- FORGIVE: to give up resentment or claim to requital for insult; to cease to feel resentment against an offender (http://www.merriam-webster.com/)

- TO WIPE THE SLATE CLEAN (allabout God.com)

> *But if ye forgive not men their trespasses,*
> *neither will your Father forgive your trespasses.*
>
> —Matthew 6:15 (KJV)

- MERCY: Compassionate treatment, clemency, kind and forgiving (dictionary.search.yahoo.com)

> *And David said unto God, I am in a great strait:*
> *let me fall now into the hand of the LORD;*
> *for very great are his mercies:*
> *but let me not fall into the hand of man.*
>
> —1 Chronicles 21:13 (KJV)

- GRACE: To honor or favor … unmerited divine assistance given humans for their regeneration or sanctification (http://www.merriam-webster.com/)

> *For by grace are ye saved through faith;*
> *and that not of yourselves:*
> *it is the gift of God:*[9]
> *Not of works, lest any man should boast.*
>
> —Ephesians 2:8-9 (KJV)

TIPS:
- FORGIVENESS does not mean that you will always forget whatever

happened to you—after all, that's the point: "It happened to you!" You may not have been as vigilant, or you may have chosen bad situations, or you may have been blinded about a person, situation, bad habit, or addiction yourself! But some act or acts have happened to you that you are now charged to forgive.

- FORGIVENESS does not mean that you condone the hurtful behavior of someone, but that you choose to have empathy and to release the judgment and penalty or revenge toward that person.

- FORGIVENESS can help the offender truly repent and change and can even lead to reconciliation. You can't change the person or undo what happened, but forgiveness can help put the past in perspective and in a context that leads to healing. The emotional pain will then decrease.

> *Remember ye not the former things,*
> *neither consider the things of old.[19]*
> *Behold, I will do a new thing;*
> *now it shall spring forth;*
> *shall ye not know it?*
> *I will even make a way in the wilderness,*
> *and rivers in the desert.*
>
> —Isaiah 43:18–19 (KJV)

- SOMETIMES, we can get stuck in the anger and bargaining phase of loss when we're working on forgiveness. It is important to come to grips with the fact that the past cannot be undone. It is such a simple statement but so hard to disconnect in your heart and mind. However, it helps greatly if the person who hurt you can say, "I wish I could undo what I did to hurt you"—AND REALLY MEAN IT! Of course, God knows our hearts.

- REALIZE that God has "let go" of your mistakes and He has "let go" of the mistakes of others against you. His Son, Jesus, walked the earth in forgiveness. Think of the betrayers and sinners he met:

Judas, Peter, Paul, and Mary Magdalene, to name a few.

Never does the human soul appear so strong
as when it foregoes revenge and dares to forgive an injury

—Edwin Hubbel Chapin

• STAY mindful that some people may use and manipulate a forgiving spirit for their own gains. Check yourself for codependent behaviors. Are you so needy that you find yourself always bonding to people who have problems and take advantage of you? Read the book *Foolproofing Your Life: An honorable way to deal with the impossible people in your life* (1998), by Jan Silvious. It is based on Proverbs and helps with all relationships.

• MERCY goes hand in hand with empathy. It means to see and feel what someone says and does in a manner that allows "walking in their shoes." Are you able to feel that other person's pain or struggle? Your mercy alone may open their eyes!

The essence of justice is mercy.

—Edwin Hubbel Chapin

• MERCY is sometimes shown by letting the offense and the person go.
• RECIPROCATE: give out the mercy you have received to others.

Not by works of righteousness which we have done,
but according to his mercy he saved us,
by the washing of regeneration,
and renewing of the Holy Ghost.

—Titus 3:5 (KJV)

GRACE FLOWS WITH MERCY!

GOD gives it to us for our regeneration.
GRACE is FREE and must also be given freely by us to others.
NO QUID PRO QUO with grace!

NO BLACKMAIL over the offender!

WHEN WE RECEIVE GOD'S GRACE, none of us totally deserves it—that is why it is called "unmerited favor."

WHY IS GRACE AMAZING? It will give you energy, a feeling of cleansing and unconditional love.

And he said unto me, My grace is sufficient for thee:
for my strength is made perfect in weakness.
Most gladly therefore will I rather glory in my infirmities,
that the power of Christ may rest upon me.

—2 Corinthians 12:9 (KJV)

So What Happened to Our Sweetheart Marriage?

By John R. Helton, Sr.

꙳

For every one that doeth evil hateth the light,
neither cometh to the light,
lest his deeds should be reproved.[21]
But he that doeth truth cometh to the light,
that his deeds may be made manifest,
that they are wrought in God.

—John 3:20-21 (KJV)

Darkness = Secrets. But Light = Truth!

Anne will tell you the miracle part of our story, of how our hearts were torn apart and how through our major *Heart Lesson* we both found God and a real relationship with his Son, Jesus.

However, I want to say first, "I do now and will forever love my Annie. The actions that tore us apart are clear now, and they were mine and mine alone."

I spent most of my life working, studying, and raising a family. Parenthood and marriage were on the job experiences for me. I was a very responsible father, but I can see my mistakes now. I would have loved to have had the advice that is available today and especially someone to call on for that advice. Often, when friends and relatives who were in a troubled relationship would ask me for advice, I would tell them they needed to work it out by talking to the partner or mate, and that other people would not have the answers, including me. I would say that if they could not solve their issues they would be destined to repeat them in another relationship. Sadly, several of those couples did divorce.

What I didn't know then and do know now is that there was someone they could talk to, and there was someone I could have called upon also for advice—God.

My problems surfaced when our children were almost grown and I had loaned a friend more money than I could afford to lose. He had guaranteed the loan with a handshake and a promise to sell his house, if needed. I know now that was risky behavior on my part and part of my problem. Then he lost the money on a bad business venture and, as it turned out, he didn't even own his home.

I felt embarrassed and sad about this failed decision I made. I kept those feelings hidden. But little did I realize, that was only the beginning. I saw a commercial on television for gold and silver investing and, strange as it may seem, I set out a course then to recoup my money losses. Unknown to me, my feelings of loss and sadness had awakened a sleeping monster of compulsive behaviors inside me. Any and all of my compulsive behaviors came together as a perfect storm, and I quickly became a compulsive gambler using the vehicle of commodity investing and trading. The type of gambling is of no consequence; they all have the same outcome. However, this type can appear more socially acceptable for a longer period of time.

I suffered from this compulsive disease for many years and spent a lot of mental and emotional energy trying to silently overcome it, and keep it hidden, only to spiral up and down on a painful internal ride. It's not an excuse but an explanation; this stronghold opened the door for me to make other wrong choices and become a person I was not proud to be. Addictions create chemical changes in the brain and can elevate a depression. They can take one into places of escape, and they come in many forms: food, fame, work, substance abuse, alcohol, sex, gambling, Internet porn, and even too much exercise.

For some people, addictive behaviors can cross over and mix with other obsessive compulsive behaviors, such as overcleanliness or hoarding. Some behaviors never progress to create external harm, but my gambling addiction caused me to act out in ways I was ashamed of and not part of my real character. Most addictions are like that, other character defects emerge, causing great shame. I was lost in my secret world, but the action of it lifted me from the depression of financial losses. It was a vicious cycle.

I always worked hard in my business and paid all of our bills and obligations; however, this actually allowed me to continue living in the sickness for years. I could keep the reality of it secret. I would rationalize that I wasn't hurting anyone but myself; however, year after year I would lose any of the funds I made, especially money that should have been set aside for our future years. I explained it away with excuses, digging my pit deeper. There had been far too many times that we had "lost everything in a risky trial." It meant the loss of money we had worked too hard to earn.

I know now that when someone is captured by the stronghold of a compulsion, everything surrounding the issue is twisted, delusional. In a gambling stronghold, the desire to win the big prize supersedes the daily grind of regular work, even if the daily work brings in plenty of money. I know, it doesn't make sense—but that's the point! It's a high in the brain, much like cocaine, and the behavior, just as with Sisyphus of Greek mythology is as much about the struggle up the hill as it is in the fall back down. Strange as it sounds, the high can be addictive coming and going.

For some people, like me, starting over was a purge of sorts, a making of a clean slate. But then the climb up the hill began again. It can also be said that the constant pushing and toiling of pushing a rock up a hill, only to have it roll back down or over the edge, is an accepted internal punishment that someone might inflict on themselves. But this could really only be done by someone who has no hope, mainly no belief in mercy, forgiveness, redemption. It's actually a climb within a road rut so deep that getting out, when possible, requires a shock, a pain—a truck hitting you on that road!

John faces hill

With any type of gambling—poker, casino, lottery, sports, trading—the "secret" is tightly guarded for several reasons: The gambler doesn't want to or can't stop; they have shame about their actions, their losses. Also, we are delusional about the extent of the problem; and we also believe, (I really believed), that we will hit it big and be able to make up all the losses and redeem ourselves—financially, that is!

Without recovery, redemption becomes about filling the internal empty pit with money, but the real void is spiritual emptiness. Like most compulsive gamblers, my actions eventually caused our world to fall apart. I couldn't keep the spiraling money loss a secret anymore, and my inner world was coming apart. I was devastated, as I always felt strongly about never knowingly causing anyone problems. But here I was becoming one. I thought I could never be vindictive or selfish, but now I was. And I had let down and destroyed my most important relationship of all, my Annie. She is the core of my life, and I hurt her terribly. She was never about money, but she could no longer handle the secret life of the compulsive gambling roller-coaster ride, or especially the information I dumped on her about character flaws in earlier years. While I needed to purge, I realize now I also used it as a deflection. It crushed her, and I am so sorry.

I had lied to her, but mostly to myself. She eventually left me, and I was then all alone to ponder my life. I was still in the grip of my gambling addiction, and as most gamblers I was certain that I could fix our marriage with just a few good commodity trades! I worked my real job night and day, but I also traded long hours each day. (My trading was via the old-fashioned method, on the phone; however, the Internet has made it even more deadly for compulsive traders today.) I was making money, and I thought this would fix everything! Character issues and spirituality were not even on my radar! I was in a fog.

And then it happened—the doorbell rang, and a man served me with final papers. My Annie had actually divorced me! I read the papers in disbelief. Our forty-seven years of marriage were over!

This got my attention. I was lost and desperate. I felt totally alone. I looked at myself and didn't like what I saw. I felt such despair and loneliness, and only a few people came to see me or called. While I appreciated and embraced them, I felt confused and ashamed. I learned later that I had abandonment issues as a child; thus, being all alone now confirmed my worst fears. And Annie would not come home.

In my despair, I picked up the Bible I had in the house and actually read it. I started to volunteer at St. Vincent de Paul to sit in the chapel at night, and I joined St. Luke Methodist's men's group. I spent a lot of time reading spiritual books at "St. Barnes and Noble" too! It took losing Annie to wake me up. However, a very huge step was to divest myself from any trading or "investing," to cut all ties and close all accounts with brokers, and to join Gamblers Anonymous (GA) and take the first step of surrendering to my Higher Power.

I was thus beginning the most important step of my life toward my own health. GA meetings are available everywhere, and they were right in front of me all along, but I wasn't ready. Through participation and perseverance at GA meetings, and with God's help, Annie and I started to really talk and see each other differently, and I became healthy. I understand my character flaws and my feelings now. I know how to handle them, and I know how to pray. We were blessed with our own resurrection. I thank God daily for giving me the grace of another chance, and for the actual miracle that happened one Sunday when my Annie came to give me another chance! ✥

What shall we then say to these things?
If God be for us, who can be against us?

—Romans 8:31 (KJV)

Twelve Stepping Stones
to Character

By Anne Stewart Helton

Anne faces stepping stones

By whom also we have access by faith into this grace
wherein we stand,and rejoice in hope of the glory of God.[3]
And not only so, but we glory in tribulations also:
knowing that tribulation worketh patience;[4]
And patience, experience; and experience, hope:[5]
And hope maketh not ashamed; because the love
of God is shed abroad in our hearts
by the Holy Ghost which is given unto us.

—Romans 5:2–5 (KJV)

"You mean I'm supposed to go to a twelve-step program too? NO WAY! That's insane!" I said to the lady as I slammed down the phone.

My husband of forever had just hit the proverbial bottom and faced the reality that his years of "investing" was actually compulsive gambling. So, we were broke and in trouble with debt—again. It was painful to the core and extremely confusing to me. I had heard about all the typical gambling problems and had actually seen some glazed bingo gamblers in my childhood who had to be dragged from fall festivals. I had also seen raffle ticket junkies and later lottery ticket buyers in daily lines at the grocery store. But investing? Everyone does that, right?

But for me, when I realized he had hit bottom, this time, what it really meant was, "It was over." "It" meant that hell was getting ready to rain down on us—again. I had no way of knowing how, but I knew it meant that I was getting off the merry-go-round, and off the roller coaster! The pain of John's compulsive gambling and investing had reared its ugly head again, and this time I was AWAKE!

As is common in almost all compulsions or addictions, the partner or family is unaware of the full reality. But gambling can be one of the hardest to detect or face. So much of the behavior is acceptable in society, and if the method is "investing, day trading, online trading, or commodity trading," it almost seems un-American not to do it. Often, the brokers involved in the trading may even realize their

Midnight grief

customer is addicted, but they make money on every trade, in and out, so they often look the other way. One of the fastest types of gambling now is sports betting, and many young college students are lured into the trap only to find they are susceptible to gambling addictions—in a short time they have thousands of dollars of credit card debt! It's all about the action—all about the play. With the explosion of social

135

media, it's easier than ever to get a "hit" off of the play, and each "hit" is a high that builds the appetite for more and more.

Oh, the *dark places* this stronghold will take you, and the midnights you will visit. . . .

The problem for us started years before this current crisis, when John started buying commodities, specifically silver, right after he lost thousands investing with a "friend" for an invention; which was after he had lost thousands in a loan to a "friend" who wanted to sell player pianos; which was after we had sold our house to pay off debts from credit cards for the friends; which was—well, you get the picture. Everything and everyone he "invested in" always hooked his wanting to help the person. It was not to "get rich quick," but he wanted to be the hero—classic symptoms we know now of low self-esteem and codependency.

And where was I during this tragic play? Living my own career with my head clearly in the sand, and believing every word of what my husband told me—because I wanted to believe, regardless of any reality in front of me. Ugh!

I never realized he had what is now termed a "compulsive problem." Some compulsions are good (organized people), but I never realized that compulsions could also be on a continuum, that is, become worse or switch to other obsessions. Sometimes, when he was mad at himself, he would "pick a verbal fight." I know now that was a "gambler's game" to "get the monkey off his back" about whatever he was upset about internally. He would always apologize. I made allowances instead of boundaries; we both used *denial* like a drug and didn't confront the big issues like we should have. It was much like an alcoholic who will avoid facing the "elephant in the room," and will walk around it and just keep on drinking.

It was when our children left home that we first realized that John's loaning or investing with friends for *their* business ideas and "commodity investing" may be compulsive gambling. We went to a few meetings of Gamblers Anonymous at St. Michael's Church, and I also tried to address the issue with a therapist, but John believed he could battle it on his own and that it wasn't really a huge problem. I easily bought that too. After all, he had done it before, and no way did I want to address that real elephant!

We just kept on going through the years; and a lot of them were very good years of work, careers, kids, family, fun—LIFE!

So, we continued to lose money off and on but we made a lot of money too—in the *real* jobs! Our children were grown and into their own careers and lives, and we rocked along in ours, living more or less in our own worlds.

Also, I was deep into caring for my father who had Alzheimer's. We both helped my mom provide care for him and we were often at their house, late, every night, as he progressed in the disease. John would often take my father to work with him, creating little jobs for him, and thus allowing him to still have some dignity from work. My dad would have his hat and sweater-vest on, stand outside on Buffalo Speedway, and eagerly wait for John to pick him up for "work." It was so kind.

In March of 2006, and then December of 2006 (same year), John lost his father, and then his mother. They were WWII, Depression-era, good people. He seemed to be worse about his compulsions and moods after that. I noticed his emotions were more labile, and he seemed more depressed and angry. I felt we were disconnected emotionally.

On July 11, 2008, my father died. My world seemed to fall apart, like an out-of-orbit, spinning solar system. I was his firstborn, and he was always available to me.

Maxine and Bill Helton and dog "Sugar"

This had a huge emotional impact on John too, as we both loved him and had spent many hard years caring for him in his declining years of dementia. What I didn't know at that time was that John was

137

Anne with father, 1947

in a death spiral with compulsive gambling. He worked day and night to make money but would never just put it in the bank and save it. He craved the action of "investing" (gambling) and that was his drug. So he would always create situations to make himself have the action; then he could work harder to make the money to invest more. It was a mental high. It sounds crazy—because it was!

On a November night in 2008, I was working on the computer and went into the other room to find John in his chair, staring ahead. He looked in a lot of pain and was speaking very quietly. He said he had lost everything again, that we were heavy in debt and had no savings left either. He said he had used it all to try again on an investment, doesn't matter which one—coffee, soybeans, coal, oil—it was compulsive gambling. He said he thought he could make it up (again), but I knew things were really bad.

My veil of denial was finally ripped off. I had NO energy left to repeat the cycle again. We were no longer communicating normally at all.

Even though I worked with him, side by side, I knew I would no longer do that again. I was crying about our situation, but mostly I think because I knew it was over—I couldn't do the money cycle again. But I was crying about my age (sixty-two); how would I get back into nursing? How could we survive? We had nothing left.

I knew things were bad, but little did I know that night that I would be kicked in the gut with John's decision to purge himself about an earlier period of our marriage (Or was he trying to manipulate me and deflect me from his money issue, and keep me from talking about compulsive gambling?) It was like God was hitting me with everything bad at once! John seemed to be unable to stop the words from coming out, and he confessed bad character flaws he had during earlier parts of our marriage and how sorry he was.

I couldn't even comprehend WHAT he was saying. Nor did I think

John realized what his "revelations" would do to me. He was only thinking of himself, and he felt better because he had "confessed." I don't think he realized how much I valued our wedding vows. And, as he said, "after all, it was a long time ago." All those years, and he had neatly compartmentalized and rationalized his early behaviors. I had been clueless!

I felt so worthless and blamed myself. I felt I wasn't enough for him! I put it all on myself instead of realizing it was his problem. I felt like a crazy person.

I started planning what to do—that night. I couldn't believe what was happening to my life. I felt that I had been living for years with a complete stranger.

John felt better getting it all *off his chest*, but then all he wanted to do was bargain and stuff feelings back in the bottle. He wanted to work hard again and make money, begging to "invest," he said, just ten percent of any money we could make again. It was the Sisyphus story again. It was absolutely crazy. I think he really believed if he could make a bunch of money that I would be okay; as if I would forget everything

I spiraled into hell because my world was falling apart. Trying to still save John and our marriage, I was up all night on the computer reading about marriage counseling, about addictions, about gambling.... I found the *Retrouvaille* marriage program online and called the intake couple. They had been through a tough period too and helped me a lot by listening, which allowed me to see I wasn't crazy. They also said there was HOPE.

But have you ever cried so hard you were blind? I mean flooding, flowing, wailing tears? I'm talking about the kind of tears that wipe you out like a marathon. Or dripping tears on a keyboard. Getting those tears out is critical, but *oh, my Lord*, they sure can mess up your face! That was ME!

Anne's tears on keyboard

139

I registered us for the *Retrouvaille* marriage help program and we were set to go, but GOD helped me to realize that unless John confronted his compulsive "demons" and his past, and unless I was not in as much pain from the secrets, we were not ready for a weekend encounter. We had serious, serious problems. I felt God made John "spill his guts" to me to wake me up. I needed to stop trying to fix our marriage. God opened my eyes to this fact. Somehow God gave me the strength and discernment to pray, pray, pray, and to realize that I had to "let go and let God" deal with the issues. I cried out to God, and HE answered me—it was personal.

I slept VERY little but I had so much energy it was amazing! I still tried and tried to find out more about the past that I had not been privy to. I spent countless hours obsessing. I just needed the truth and felt completely untrusting of John. I wanted to hear other people tell me everything, and I wanted to scream at them about how they ruined my life. I even walked into an anonymous brokerage company and yelled at some poor brokers. They stared at me as I turned and walked out, slamming the door! I'm sure the phrase "some crazy lady" was uttered!

John made an appointment for us with a parish priest, but all I did was cry, and he thought it would magically "fix me." I felt manipulated by his use of the church. The priest was kind and said some good things, but I couldn't "hear" him.

My need to know the facts became obsessive. I have since learned that is typical!

We began to have major fights and some turned physical. I broke many plates and threw everything I could whenever I felt like it. As far as the Grief cycle, it was clear that I was stuck in anger. John cried and screamed for me to stop asking him about everything he had blurted out to me. He actually seemed confused about it also, couldn't remember, and seemed to be exaggerating at times to get me off the topic of the loss of money. I learned later that he was very confused, but at the time I didn't believe him.

It began to get dangerous because I was fighting more now. No longer afraid of his assertive personality or refusal to talk, I would push and push. This is typical for the spouse of a compulsive gambler. I also felt my father's boxing skills in my own body, and I believed, if needed, I could beat the hell out of John. Never in my life had I ever, ever been that way, but I wanted him to hurt like he had hurt me. Actually, I wanted to die. I think without God's help it would have been devastating for both of us. I felt dead already. I mean, it's pretty low down when your own grandchildren hear you humming AC/DC's "*Dirty Deeds Done Dirt Cheap*"!

One of the very real spiritual moments that happened to me occurred late at night. I was awake, lying in bed, doing my usual—crying and praying. John was sound asleep, which made me angrier. I felt I saw my dead father sitting down on my bed next to me. He reached over and put his arm around my shoulder closest to John and rolled me away from him, as if I was being unyoked. I instantly felt relief; and I knew then I WAS LEAVING! I was leaving the love of my life.

While John was busy "trying to make more money," I packed our whole house in boxes all by myself. I rented a storage room too. He was so addicted to gambling and trying to make money to buy another commodity contract that he really didn't notice my packing.

Packed boxes

Like any addict, he was so used to blocking feelings that he didn't see me and my pain.

I totally knew then that he was sick. I felt like a "lamp" to him. I was the "lamp" in the house that he turned on when *he* wanted light.

I was slowly moving boxes to my mother's townhouse, and John would comment on how nicely I was "decluttering" the house. His reaction actually helped me to realize how delusional he was about our situation and his problems. I felt calmer. I understood more.

Anne drives off

So, on a cold day in February, I moved out. It was two and a half months after he told me about his secrets. I had made it through Thanksgiving, Christmas, and New Year's, and I wanted to somehow survive. I drove off with the last of my things in my car and went to my mother's after forty-seven years of marriage!

I remember he came outside and stood on the front porch and said, "Where are you going?" *I just drove off.*

This still did not wake John up, because he thought I would be home in a few days. But I didn't leave to wake him up. I had finally realized that I had to leave for me—to help me survive, to rebuild my own character.

Over the next several months, I attended Gamanon support-group meetings for spouses of compulsive gamblers. I learned as much as I could about the problem and my role in the denial. With support letters from old colleagues, I restructured my career, updated my resume, took necessary update courses, got immunizations, and more. I went to a therapist, a business lawyer, an old district attorney friend for wisdom, and I started seeing a psychologist to help me with the sleepless nights filled with visions and tears from a broken heart.

I felt so bad about myself as a woman and wife that I marched into Victoria's Secret, bought way too much perfume and every color of lacy lingerie—I even bought a thong! Sexy? Maybe? But honestly, it was the most uncomfortable item I've ever worn!

I tried to sell all the jewelry John had ever bought me, but I met the nicest older man who tried to talk me into packing it away. He said he had been through "red hot emotional pain" before and that it could get better. I laughed in his face, but I did pack it away!

I had many sleepless nights living at my mom's. Sometimes I would

142

walk outside alone, late at night, or lie down in bed and then get up and go sit in the closet, pull out boxed-up towels from my house, and just smell them. I don't know why, but I could smell the memories, the loving times, and just remember that I was once whole and happy. I have heard that often happens in grief with the death of a spouse.

It seems silly now, but I have always had a great sense of smell; and often my life memories were tied to them. Like Old Spice cologne. Whenever I smelled that cologne, I could see my father shaving in the morning, getting ready for work. I could automatically go back to Oak Forest and hear mother telling everyone to get up, eat, and get ready for school. So when I smelled the towels from my life with John, I remembered more of the good than the bad. I started to actually realize that there was much more good than bad..

I knew I was *shifting,* but I didn't understand it!

He had been a geology major in college, and I remembered the trips to the Hill Country to hunt for shark's teeth or fossils. Whenever John learned something new, he loved to take me and our children, or anyone, with us, to experience it. He was a natural-born teacher. We would take whatever money we could scrape up for gas and trek off to walk through creek beds in Austin, Hills in Bedias, or walk through water at Honey Creek by Llano Texas. Back in those days one could just stop the car and get out for a hike. Sometimes, the property owners would even be aware but just nod at hikers as they trudged through their property. As long as one left it like it was, there was usually no problem.

We would walk by watery trails and see glimpses of shiny "gold," and the kids would stop, suddenly thinking they had found treasure. Then John would teach us all about feldspar or mica and how iron pyrite fooled many people who

John rock hunting

143

John and Grandson Matt feed turtles

thought it was real gold. We would find fossils, and he would tell stories of the American Cherokee Indians, his actual ancestors, who camped along the hills, and how they hunted for their own food, protected the land, and never wasted anything they found or killed.

He taught the children to carry out whatever they brought onto the land, to respect nature, and that hunting should be for food or survival. It would be unusual for him to step on a bug just to kill it or to kill a snake or anything. He had a healthy respect for snakes! Basically, he didn't believe in harming anything that just wanted to live and didn't attack first.

I remembered when he fed the turtles in the neighborhood creek fresh apples every day, how he wore silly ties with the grandsons and our son-in-law on Thanksgivings, as well as when he held

Grandad, little Molly and Casey on treasure hunt

legendary treasure hunts for our children and grandchildren who had big imaginations. So many shared adventures!

Wearing silly ties at Thanksgiving

He taught our children to listen to the wind, to read the stars, and to wonder about life and where it came from. We often talked about God, having baptized both children, but we didn't have a personal God relationship. We lived the '60s and '70s lifestyle of philosophy, ethics, and sometimes agnosticism.

WHAT A MAJOR MISTAKE!

One night, while sitting alone in my mom's closet, I saw my flat dancing shoes stuffed in a box—old, scuffed black ballet-type shoes. I remembered the times I would say bossily to John, who was basically shy in a crowd, "Just dance. Who cares how you look?" Once, at a family wedding I complained to others: How could he or anyone not get up and dance to the song "Shout"? *Oh, this was going to be a long wedding reception,* I remembered.

My whole family ALWAYS danced to-gether to "Shout". And after the last "little bit louder now", Richard, #3 would start his James Brown guttural "Heys" and walk reluctantly off the dance floor to cheers and calls for more! All my brothers could perform, from Walter, #4 and his great guitar notes, to Jimmy, #9 and Billy, #10, with their good singing voices, dancing and impersonation skills.. It was just

Anne and Brother Richard dance

crazy fun, but it must have looked like a well-staged performance on Broadway to someone like John who did not like to be in the lime-light, as did my family of origin. *I should have understood that!*

I actually enjoyed the way my husband danced when we were alone at home, in our kitchen, but he became practiced at sitting out these public displays. I tried not to make him feel left out, but the truth was I pouted. I wanted him out there, with me—being like me.

Sadly, I remembered many times judging him for not being just like my family of origin.

John had the dancing joy in him and loved music. In fact, when our children were small, he would put on music from old sound tracks, like "Paint Your Wagon." He loved to sing and dance with them, belting out having been born "under a wandering star." They loved it, and I would watch fondly as they stomped around blankets on the floor piled up like a campfire singing "No Name City." Life felt good for us in those private moments of joy.

But I wanted my partner to dance with me. So, if we were at a party or event he would, but I could always tell it was difficult for him. Once, when we were in Montreal at a club, I just got up and danced with some perfect stranger! I looked over and watched my husband as he monitored where the guy's limbs were at all times, and I just danced and danced and danced. Afterwards, he genuinely said, "Did you have fun?"

Actually, I'm sure I looked like a child having a temper tantrum. I wanted what I wanted. But he was just happy that I was happy.

Through the years of our marriage, many of our differences, like dancing, rose to the top; but mostly we liked the same things and had the same interests in life. However, I know now we needed to talk about our feelings more, and our real issue was that we didn't have God in our lives in any substantial sense. Our marriage had no spiritual foundation for times of real trouble, and it rolled along on rocky soil and on a bumpy road until we went off into the ditch—and we crashed.

It's funny, but the night that I decided I had to leave my husband after forty-seven years of marriage, the strangest thing was I had gotten out of bed and gone into our living room, I was listening to the Rolling Stones playing loudly, and again I was crying and dancing at 2:00 a.m. I was a mess.

He was asleep. He escaped. I acted out.

Our marital demise had become a dark, deep hole—for both of us. As he faced his issues and hit bottom when I left, I also faced myself and my need for some changes. The grieving was immeasurable. We had been together since high school; we were ripped in half. We were so sad.

So, when I found myself split from my life mate and alone, I began to reach out more and more to God. I desperately wanted to know that someone really cared about me and would carry me through the pain I was feeling. I listened to ALL of Redeemer Presbyterian Church, Tim Keller's podcast (www.redeemer.com) which helped me understand God more, as well as the wise words of Max Lucado (maxlucado.com). I bought many books to read about Jesus—mainly daily inspirational books; and I read and reread Beth Moore's book, *Get out of that Pit*. In so many ways these readings were foreign to me. I read what Beth wrote, "you can't get yourself out of a pit" and "you can't trust man to be your God". She stated that people may help you out of a pit but they can't keep you out, only God can do that. That began to sink in for me. (Used with permission of the author, Beth Moore,"Get Out of That Pit")

I had never believed that I could actually *talk personally* with Jesus. It seemed that night time, especially about 4:00 a.m., was always the worse when I was away from John. I have heard others in pain say the same about that time of the morning. Once, while praying for solace, I asked God to show me he was there.

Deep down inside I heard these two words: "I AM." I sat straight up in bed and looked around. I was still alone.

Still trying to learn the Bible, I had no idea what the words meant. I called my brother-in-law, Doctor Mark Jacobs, a self-taught Old and New Testament scholar, the next day, and he explained how in Exodus 3:14 God said to Moses, "*I AM WHO I AM. This is what you are to say to the Israelites: 'I AM has sent me to you.'*"

My brother-in-law was floored about what I heard in my heart also, and then he humbly asked me, "What did God sound like?" I loved this because it made it even more real to me.

"Well," I said, "He sounded like…well…He sounded like God!"

It was then that I knew—*I knew*—that I knew God was real and that He was with me! I knew He must have a plan for the pit I was in. I just didn't know yet how I would get out or what the plan would or could possibly be!

BUT GOD DID!

So, I filed for divorce. I helped to write my own divorce papers. I had a tough attorney, but I told her I didn't want to "destroy" John, but I knew I needed to wake him up or move on myself to survive. Incidentally, her degree was in philosophy, and she knew all about Sisyphus's struggles too.

I started working in teaching and nursing again, and gently I took care of myself. My children were worried about me but knew I did not want to remain a "victim." My daughter was amazing as she struggled to help me heal while deep in her heart she was hurting for her father. Her husband Larry cried for the pain John was going through also. My son, sadly, was stuck in anger, but I know now that anger is a secondary emotion. He tried, but he was probably hurting too.

My siblings seemed to grieve also, as they had grown up with John. There was plenty of confusion and anger to go around. I found comfort in living with and helping my mom, who had health issues, and also finally grieving my father's death (which had been interrupted with my life crisis).

My wise #7 sibling, Julie, kept me connected to Bible studies, and John and I fought all the time via e-mails and phone calls. Still, we always managed to "run into each other" at the grocery store, where they always seem to play those old love songs over the loud speakers, which made me cry conspicuously while I was shopping. We would see each other when out walking for exercise or when going to Mass at church. It made me furious because he would hold my hand during the *Lord's Prayer* and ask me to "try to forget the past."

I knew he had compartmentalized everything due to his own shame or guilt, but that didn't help me. I wanted repentance—actually, I admit, I still wanted *blood*.

I called John the night before my divorce court date, wanting to see real character change, but I still didn't feel it was there. I was so focused on the percentage of hurt in our marriage that I refused to look at the larger percentage of goodness and love. So, on July 15, 2009, we were divorced. I stood in front of the family court judge, and my marriage was over too quickly—forty-seven years wiped off the books!

I was so sad, but I knew I had taken a necessary step for my survival.

From the day John received the real divorce papers in the mail, August 15, 2009, he seemed to wake up. The pain in his voice was palpable. I was at work, and he called me over and over, trying to reach me to talk. He was hurting, and I could hear it. I was stunned that it took such severe action to open his heart. Much as I wanted desperately to run to his arms, I had learned from wise counsel to watch what he DID, not what he SAID. I had received good advice on boundaries: "Watch the feet, not the mouth."

I had to fight to stay away from him.

By the end of the summer of 2009, John and I were in discovery, individual therapy, Bible groups, lots of crying, fighting, grieving, and—what I realize now—still *hanging on* to each other. I had joined a great divorce support group at Second Baptist, but I just never felt connected to the people. Our stories were similar, but I guess the truth was, I really didn't feel divorced. Some of the hurting men were exploring relationships with me, but I didn't feel connected to them either.

John was going religiously to his Gamblers Anonymous (GA) meetings, but I didn't really trust him or myself yet. I felt he was still playing a "game" and trying to "win" me back. All I thought about was why was I so stupid to have believed his plans about "investing" for years? I hated and loved him at the same time. I actually prayed for God to hurt him as much as I was hurting.

Even though I went to churches all over town for comfort, I also went out some nights, often alone. My words of pain were unfiltered and I ran my *entitled* mouth off to everyone who couldn't run away from me—especially waiters at a bar! I was fueled by my emotions. I was not careful with my words at all and talked endlessly about my pain, which gave people around me future fuel for their own hurtful words. I defined "pity party".

I never was a "drinker," but I tried drinking margaritas to "find myself" but really it was just to escape the pain. AND IT DOESN'T WORK! And besides, then you have a headache on top of the emotional pain!

This was not me at all. I finally faced how much of my whole being was trapped inside of my husband. I thought more about him than God or myself, and I started to change that behavior. God had to become FIRST in my life. I walked miles and miles listening to different preacher tapes and music I prayed the Rosary and asked God over and over to fix my heart.

John kept trying to be nice—and he was so all alone in our old house. I felt so bad for him because he had lost everything, just like a guy at a casino, but by now I realized that it was all his choice, and only he could change his life. Our empathetic daughter was kind to him but hurting too. He was alone every night, but God was reaching him too. He was reading the Bible, going to men's groups, and the GA twelve-step group meetings.

John was finding his inner strength and real self. He showed actual behavior change now. I was starting to feel my heart soften too, but then I was surprised because I could tell God was making me feel kinder toward John. Then I would feel angry: *Why should I forgive him?* I prayed constantly for discernment. What was God's will for me—for US?

We were actually divorced now, so why couldn't I move on? Was this a chance to get it right, to get even, or were we supposed to move on, as our culture and media prescribed for troubled marriages? Was I full of pride?

I cried out "Why Me, God?" but then I realized WHY NOT ME? Many couples had problems; we weren't superior or immune from trials.

Almost one year from when our marriage blew up, I heard from a friend in a Beth Moore Home Bible class about the Australian singer, Darlene Zschech, who was to be singing at Lakewood Church in Houston. I invited John to go with me. *Uh-Oh!?* What could that hurt, right? We had never been to Lakewood Church, but we both liked watching Pastor Joel Osteen on TV.

I wasn't sure what to expect, but by now my heart was raw and open to whatever the Holy Spirit blew down on me. I was ready for anything. So we went. John was trying so hard to be nice, but we were tense in the car the whole way there, I almost got out of the car. It really seemed on that Sunday that we would just go and at least learn to be friends but stop trying to reconcile. I actually said, "Maybe I'll meet a man!"

The only way to describe the service was awesome. We ended up praying with a prayer partner named Lynn Parks (I had never done anything like that before). Pastor Joel wasn't supposed to even be there that day but, unexpectedly he was, so that was incredible too. As first-time attendees, we had been seated at the very front of the church by the friendly ushers. The whole Osteen family was welcoming and spiritual.

By the time the service ended we were holding hands. We didn't want to stop touching. His hand was warm.

When it was time to leave, John asked if I wanted to try to find my Bible-class friend to "thank her" for recommending the service. We walked the aisles and tried to find her in the 16,000-person crowd, with no success. We stepped up on some stairs to search and then decided to just e-mail her later.

While walking down the steps, I turned around and literally bumped into Pastor Joel Osteen. (If you were visiting Lakewood you would know how rare that would be!)

After we both apologized to each other, I was shaken. It was as if God defibrillated my heart. Joel talked to John specifically, and when he heard how much he was hurting and how long we had been married, and that we were now divorced, he stopped everything and prayed with us. He had tears in his eyes and prayed for God to heal our hearts. Then he asked us to please "come with him." We followed him and his security team through a maze of stairs and ended up with what seemed like thousands of people waiting for him to sign his new book, *It's Your Time*.

Instead, for a few minutes, people waited as Pastor Joel talked privately with us and listened to a synopsis of our story. He prayed so hard for us. He cried with us and asked again for God to heal us. He gave John his first book, signed it, and then asked us to keep in touch.

We walked away stunned, and then of all things we saw the actual prayer partner, Lynn, with whom we had prayed during the service. We told her what had just happened with Joel, and she was tearful and amazed and asked us to spend some time with her.

We talked, cried, prayed, and then right there in the old Houston Rocket's Compaq Center, now the Lakewood Church, we both forgave and recommitted to each other and to God. My heart felt peace and forgiveness.

Yes, a miracle! With the snap of a finger, our hearts had changed and we were now going to have the *God-centered grown-up* marriage

Pastor Joel Osteen, Anne and John Helton, Lakewood Church-Houston

we always deserved with each other.

Four months later, as a special favor to us, Pastor Joel Osteen remarried us. We had been given a gift from God, through Jesus and then Joel, and we were headed towards our golden wedding anniversary, even using our testimony now to teach and heal others with hurting marriages. We learned first-hand:

You intended to harm me, but God intended it for good
to accomplish what is now being done, the saving of many lives.

—Genesis 50:20: (KJV)

So, after some very *out loud and public* pain and drama, we had sought help and found our way to God. I had gone to Lakewood Church to maybe meet a man—and I did! The road to reconciliation was totally a miracle. Through Christ and a pastor who knows how to cast a net like Peter, we had been redeemed. We were whole again and now the veils of pride, betrayal, and strongholds are gone.

We found out that *Love Is Forgiveness*. It has been well over six years now. We have seen how God moves and changes lives, sometimes in great pain, but always for the better. For some people, the change happens over time, but sometimes it happens in the "snap of a finger," as it did with us. It's all God's timing.

At service last week, our lively choir was singing about "God's Great Dance Floor," and, *believe or not,* our pastor had beachballs flowing through the crowd and a HUGE disco ball hanging down from the top of our mega church. (We believe it's okay to be happy in church.)

As the ball swirled and the lights glittered around in circles over the thousands of attendees, the music tempo rose and my body started jumping. I looked over at my husband. I saw his

Fun Lakewood Church service

arms in the air, joy on his face, and watched his feet moving beyond, beyond. No shyness. No hesitation. "Let's dance," he said, and we did.

Thou hast turned for me my
mourning into dancing:
thou hast put off my sackcloth, and
girded me with gladness.

—

Psalm 30:11 (KJV)

We never stopped going to Lakewood Church!

After all, Jesus, Joel, and Victoria Secret saved my life, and my heart had changed—with the snap of a finger that took a lifetime!

John volunteers at Lakewood Church

Celebrating Golden Anniversary

If God can do that for me, He can do it for you! For us, it was remarriage; for you, it may be a different path, but staying connected to God will keep you on the *right* path! It has been over 50 years for us now (cumulative, as we don't count the months apart, and John definitely doesn't use the "D" word—"divorce"). We are spiritually, emotionally and financially fit.

I was awakened, clearly now. My years of keeping my head in the sand were over, and it had all been *stepping stones* in the river of life to build my character too. I learned the importance of receiving and giving mercy and forgiveness, as well as the damage of being judgmental to others. God had taken us through the fire for these *heart lessons*.

God used many earth angels, churches, and spiritual leaders, and then finally Lakewood Church and Pastor Joel Osteen to open our hearts and bring us back together.

We are discovering our *gifts* from God of encouragement and teaching in marriage groups and church,God is using our *test* as a testimony for others. I have heard it said that we should all try to pass the tests God gives us in life because HIS *make-up tests* are even harder. So very true!

> *But ye shall receive power,*
> *after that, the Holy Ghost is come upon you:*
> *and ye shall be witnesses unto me both in Jerusalem,*
> *and in all Judaea, and in Samaria,*
> *and unto the uttermost part of the earth.*
> —Acts 1:8 (KJV)

Deep down, I thank God that I had realized I wanted the real John in my life, especially if we could do the hard work to have an honest, equal, and loving life together in recovery and forgiveness.

And, YES, I learned it was insane NOT to go to a twelve-step support group. I found some very wise, godly women in that group over several years. They were my stepping stones. We express gratefulness daily that we held on to the Rock of Christ in that stormy river that we both fell into. We did the hard work needed to rebuild our lives. We went back to the *Retrouvaille* marriage program and also to every program and Bible class Lakewood Church had, along with the twelve-step program groups.

We learned everything we *should* have learned many years ago, and now we share it with other hurting couples. We know that God will help anyone who hangs on to Him, and we pray for anyone who feels hopeless. I learned not to judge others and to feel a special empathy if I see a sad woman in a grocery store or a woman walking alone at night, and I pray for her.

We learned the unconditional love of Jesus at Lakewood Church, from the heritage of Pastor John Osteen, to Mrs. Dodie Osteen's healing prayers, to Doctor Paul Osteen and his family's medical missions, to Pastor Lisa Osteen Comes and Pastor John Gray's Bible services, and, of course, Pastors Joel and Victoria Osteen's constant messages of God's love and hope.

For us, it was Lakewood Church, but God can reach you anywhere, in any church or even in a cardiac care unit, a garden, a Washateria, a brickyard, a hurricane, or in a coffee shop.

We want you to know that God is refining your character during any of your storms, because YOU have *heart lessons* to learn, and your own stories to tell as witnesses to God's healing power. Connect with your local church and reach out to God's people—they need you! So often we live life backwards; however, if you put God first in everything you do, then it will all work out according to God's plans, and you will become a *Happy Jesus Whatever*!

For I know the thoughts that I think toward you, saith the LORD, thoughts of peace, and not of evil, to give you an expected end.

—Jeremiah 29:11 (KJV)

Happy Jesus Couple, John and Anne Helton

POSTSCRIPT

Well, God is still surprising me...Just as this book was ready to go to print God used an old movie as a potential heart lesson. My husband loves old movies and unbeknownst to me today he was watching his favorite one, "To Kill a Mockingbird". He told me later that he was reflecting on the many times he watched it with our children, using it as one of life's lessons on civil rights and justice. When he watched the scene of lawyer Atticus Finch standing guard at the jail and his children Scout and Jim coming to protect him from the mob, my husband said he started to cry.

So, he said he went to pray about what he wanted to do next. And again, he reached out to our son; he called him on the phone and this time he answered. They then started what can only be described as a healing dialogue. Their conversation ended with "I love you, son" and "I love you, too ,Dad".

*Helton Family: John Jr., "little Bobby";
John-Bob; Melissa "Missy" and Anne*

Twelve Happy Jesus Nurse TIPS
(For Dealing with Difficult
Heart Lessons of Any Kind)

By Anne Stewart Helton

It's a lot of work. Try not to skip steps—and hang in there.

1) RECOGNITION/REALIZATION: You may hit bottom in your own way when God unblinds you. It's a juxtaposition—SURRENDER and you will gain POWER.

2) REGRETS are painful (physically and emotionally); truths may hit you—FACE THEM but reject blaming others.

3) REPENT: Express to God and a trusted support source (be careful here) your true pain and sorrow—Surrender from your heart!

4) RECONNECT: Add some daily/hourly behaviors to reconnect with God (Bible reading, prayer, classes, church time).

5) REHABILITATION: Get well! Whatever the issue is, get spiritual counsel, go to a recovery group, exercise, meet your nutritional needs, go to therapy—just get well!

6) REPAIR: Fix the damage to your body, brain, heart, soul, mind—use Dr. Caroline Leaf's methods to "switch on your brain." http://drleaf.com/

7) RESTORE/RECONCILE relationships via amends, apologies, notes, love, and prayers—Don't push or talk too much, just PRAY!

8) RELEVANCE: Find meaning from your *heart lessons*, your own storms in life. Explore the explanations, not excuses.

9) REACH OUT: Slowly move into *being there* for others in pain or with life struggles—Volunteer!

10) REST: Recognize that everything can't be fixed at once. Beware of thinking it can! (Beware of thinking under the Pink Cloud, i.e., thinking everything is perfect too soon.)

11) RESOURCEFUL: Plan ahead. Be prepared with God's Word and prayer—as you will be tested! Evil doesn't want success!

12) REMEMBER what you have accomplished, what you have Overcome! Don't dwell on the toxic behaviors, but NEVER forget God's GRACE and MERCY toward you—and then pass it on!

Resources and Recommendations
(These helped me in my *Heart Lessons*.)

Benson, Herbert, M.D., (1996) *Timeless Healing, the POWER and BIOLOGY of BELIEF*, Scribner, New York.

Bible Gateway, a searchable online Bible: https://www.biblegateway.com/

Catholic Book of Prayers, (2001) edited by Rev. Maurus Fitzgerald, O.F.M., Catholic Book Publishing Co., New Jersey.

Gamblers Anonymous, *A Day At A Time* (1976) Hazelden, Minnesota.

Gamblers Anonymous website: http://www.gamblersanonymous.org/ga/

Keller, Tim, (2008) *The Reason for God*, Dutton, New York. Sermons and Ministry, www.redeemer.com

Leaf, Caroline, (2013) *Switch On Your Brain*, Baker Books, Michigan. www.drleaf.com

Lucado, Max, (2012) *Grace*, Thomas Nelson, Nashville, Tennessee. www.maxlucado.com

Lucetta, Erik and Sue, *Growing With Christ* classes, Lakewood Church, Houston, Texas. www.lakewoodchurch.com

Meyer, Joyce, (2002) *Be Anxious for Nothing*, Faith Words, New York.

Meyer, Joyce, *People Pleasers*, http://www.joycemeyer.org

Moore, Beth, (2007) *Get Out of that Pit*, Harper Collins Christian Publishing, New York. www.lproof.org

Neeld, Elizabeth Harper, Ph.D., (2003) *Seven Choices: Finding Day-*

light after Loss Shatters Your World, Warner Books, New York. www.elizabethharperneeld.com

Osteen, Joel, (2009) *It's Your Time*, Free Press, New York. www.joelosteen.com

Osteen, Lisa, (2012) *You Are Made for More*, Hachette Book Group. www.lisacomes.com

Retrouvaille Program, A Lifeline for Marriages: http://www.retrouvaille.org/

Silvious, Jan, (1998) *Fool-Proofing Your Life, An Honorable Way to Deal with the Impossible People in Your Life*, Waterbrook Press.

Terkeurst, Lysa, (2012) *Unglued*, Zondervan, Michigan.

Twerski, Abraham J., M.D., and Craig Nakken, (1997), *Addictive Thinking and the Addictive Personality*, MJF Books, New York.